Northwest Historical Series
XVIII

By the Same Authors

Briton C. Busch

Britain and the Persian Gulf, 1894–1914

Britain, India, and the Arabs, 1914–1921

Mudros to Lausanne: Britain's Frontier in West Asia, 1918–1923

Hardinge of Penshurst: A Study in the Old Diplomacy

Master of Desolation: The Reminiscences of Capt. Joseph J. Fuller

Alta California, 1840–1842: The Journal and Observations of William Dane Phelps, Master of the Ship Alert

The War Against the Seals: A History of the North American Seal Fishery

Frémont's Private Navy: The 1846 Journal of Capt. William Dane Phelps

"Whaling Will Never Do For Me": The American Whaleman in the Nineteenth Century

Barry M. Gough

The Royal Navy and the Northwest Coast of North America, 1810–1914: A Study of British Maritime Ascendancy

To the Pacific and Arctic with Beechey: The Journal of Lieutenant George Peard of H.M.S. Blossom, *1825–1828*

Canada

Distant Dominion: Britain and the Northwest Coast of North America, 1579–1809

Gold Rush!

Gunboat Frontier: British Maritime Authority and Northwest Coast Indians, 1846–1890

The Journal of Alexander Henry the Younger, 1799–1814

The Northwest Coast: British Navigation, Trade, and Discoveries to 1812

The Falkland Islands/Malvinas: The Contest for Empire in the South Atlantic

Fur Traders from New England

The Boston Men in the North Pacific, 1787-1800

The Narratives of
WILLIAM DANE PHELPS
WILLIAM STURGIS
&
JAMES GILCHRIST SWAN

Edited, with notes and introduction by
Briton C. Busch
and
Barry M. Gough

THE ARTHUR H. CLARK COMPANY
Spokane, Washington
1997

Arthur H. Clark Company
P.O. Box 14707
Spokane, WA 99214

LIBRARY OF CONGRESS CATALOG CARD NUMBER 96-14833
ISBN-0-87062-261-7

Library of Congress Cataloging-in-Publication Data

Phelps, William Dane, 1802-1875.
    Fur Traders from New England: the Boston men, 1787-1800: the
narratives of William Dane Phelps, William Sturgis, and James
Gilchrist Swan / edited, with notes and introduction by Briton C.
Busch and Barry M. Gough.
    p. 137   cm. —(Northwest historical series; 18)
    Includes bibliographical references and index.
    ISBN 0-87062-261-7 (alk. paper)
    1. New Englanders—Northwest Coast of North America—History—
18th century.   2. Fur trade—Northwest Coast of North America—
History—18th century.   3. Northwest Coast of North America—History.
4. Hawaii—History—To 1893.   I. Sturgis, William, 1782–1863.
II. Swan, James Gilchrist.   III. Busch, Briton Cooper.   IV. Gough, Barry M.
V. Title.   VI. Series.
F 851.5. P 49   1996   96-14833
979.5—dc20   CIP

Contents

Acknowledgements

The editors acknowledge with thanks the assistance of those institutions which made possible the publication of the documents included in this volume: the Manuscripts Division of the Bancroft Library, University of California, Berkeley; the Houghton Library of Harvard University; and the Boston Public Library, which holds the only surviving run of the Boston *Commercial Bulletin* in which "Solid Men of Boston in the Northwest" originally appeared. The descendants of Captain William Dane Phelps, above all Mrs. J.H. Lawson who placed the remaining Phelps papers at our disposal, have been most helpful. Permission to publish an extract from *The Journal of William Sturgis* was granted by Professor S.W. Jackman and Sono Nis Press. Sturgis's lecture on "The Northwest Fur Trade" is reproduced here with the permission of the Provincial Archivist of British Columbia. James Swan's "Account of Vessels Engaged in the Sea-Otter Fur-Trade...," is reproduced by permission of University of Washington Press. Finally, as always we owe substantial thanks to the library staffs of our home institutions, Colgate University and Wilfrid Laurier University.

Introduction

"Solid Men of Boston in the Northwest," the first manuscript reproduced in this volume, ranks as among the great texts of American maritime enterprise, and is published here in book format for the first time. As a reliable record of a significant chapter of Boston sea pursuits in the late eighteenth and early nineteenth century, it was recognized by Hubert Howe Bancroft, R.S. Kuykendall and the dean of Massachusetts and American maritime history, Admiral Samuel Eliot Morison.[1] The latter used "Solid Men of Boston in the Northwest" as the principal text for that chapter of his *Maritime History of Massachusetts, 1783-1860,* first published in 1921, entitled "The Northwest Fur Trade." Morison drew liberally from the manuscript's content and style. Morison's heavy use of the material has had a profound influence on how Americans and others have perceived the character and the pursuits of one of the great trades of the late eighteenth and early nineteenth centuries. Morison did not identify the author of "Solid Men of Boston in the Northwest." This is understandable by virtue of the fact that the text used by Morison and others lies unsigned and undated in the manuscripts collection of the Bancroft Library, the University of California, Berkeley.

---

[1] *The Maritime History of Massachusetts*, pp. 52-63. See also his "Boston Traders in the Hawaiian Islands, 1789-1823," *Proceedings of the Massachusetts Historical Society*, 44 (1920): 9-47; Hubert H. Bancroft, *The Northwest Coast* (History of the Pacific States of North America), San Francisco: A.L. Bancroft & Co., 1984, vol. II, pp. 130ff; R.S. Kuykendall, *The Hawaiian Kingdom*, Vol. I, *"Foundation and Transformation, 1778-1854,"* Honolulu: University Press of Hawaii, 1938, p. 51, notes 65; p. 85, note 7; and p. 86, notes 9 and 10. All sources not fully described in the notes are cited in full in this work's bibliography.

The co-editor of this present book, Briton Cooper Busch, in researching the career and writings of the Boston-born sea-captain and historian William Dane Phelps, came to the conclusion that "Solid Men of Boston in the Northwest" was without doubt from Phelps's pen.[2] Professor Busch has written that Phelps was a close friend of one of the principal informants for the text, William A. Gale, who was clerk to Captain Nathan Winship of the ship *Albatross*. Phelps supplemented Gale's text with the log of the *Albatross*, a document also referred to in Phelps's autobiography, *Fore & Aft; or Leaves From the Life of an Old Sailor, by "Webfoot"* (1871). Busch's conclusion, it is true, had been suggested earlier by Ms. Adele Ogden, pioneering scholar of the California sea-otter trade.[3] Moreover, Phelps had referred breezily in correspondence to "my account of the early men of the NW...."[4] In resurrecting what is clearly Phelps's work from its earlier versions, the editors hope to establish—or reestablish—its importance in the literature.

In the early historical literature of the Northwest Coast of North America, and in particular of the Columbia River, of Russian activities in Alaska, and of British-American rivalry in the Hawaiian Islands during the War of 1812, Phelps's "Solid Men of Boston in the Northwest" is a fundamental text. This is a general account of the interlocking trade in furs, sandalwood, metals, and other items. Phelps, like Morison, was a mariner and brought the sense of the sea to his writings. Not that he had the capacities of a Joseph Conrad or an Alan Villiers, for his literary skills did not approach greatness. Rather, he brought to his task as historian a knowing appreciation of the elements of the sea and, not least, the business acumen of a sea trader.

---

[2]Busch, ed., *Alta California, 1840-1842*: p. 38.

[3]Ibid.

[4]Phelps to H.H. Bancroft, 5 May 1872, Bancroft Papers, Bancroft Library, University of California, Berkeley, C-E 65/24.

At the outset of his text Phelps explains why he has undertaken this history. He acknowledges the debt of his age to
pioneers who made known the western shores of North
America. The record of such achievements still being largely
unwritten, he regarded it as useful to future historians and
others to present an account that would show how resource-
ful efforts, for commerce or science, had imprinted themselves on the course of the history and fortunes of the
continent. Besides these reasons there stood that natural ten-
dency to record the achievements in his own society and to
leave to posterity, and to family, literary pictures of an
achievement in which he, his friends and associates played
conspicuous roles. And finally Phelps saw the enterprises of
the Boston mariners in the Pacific and on the Northwest
Coast as part of an imperial and cultural destiny whereby on
the North Pacific shores from the Gulf of California to the
Bering Sea would be extended a civilization, energetic and
advancing, announcing a new age of progress.

Phelps's "Solid Men of Boston in the Northwest" stands in
a tradition of American historical literature that is unique
and still largely under-appreciated. The logs and journals of
mariners engaged in the sea-otter trade constitute a very rich
corpus of documents upon which such histories have been
constructed.[5] The logs of John Boit and John Haswell, for
example, are classics.[6] Although many of these logs have survived and many of them have been published, or are otherwise available to researchers, it must be remembered that
during the years that the northwest trade flourished the logs
contained precious secrets of trade advantages and corporate
alliances. The trade was a secretive business for those who
carried it on. Logs were lent to mariners outward bound on
new ventures—as guides for business and advice for naviga-

---

[5]Many of these logs and records have been used by James Gibson in his *Otter Skins,
Boston Ships, and China Goods: The Maritime Fur Trade...*
[6]In F.W. Howay, ed., *Voyages of the "Columbia"....*

tion. But only after the trade closed as unprofitable or when taken over by rivals from Canada did historians turn to the task of chronicling this aspect of commercial and national endeavors. The first historians of the trade were themselves mariners in the same line of work, and in their own time they had compiled their own logs and written their own journals.

Oddly enough, "Solid Men" is a case where a handwritten, incomplete document has superseded a published, complete version, though precisely how the transformation took place is unclear. In the production of his multi-volume histories of the west, Bancroft gathered material from far and wide; such material eventually became the nucleus of the Bancroft Library. At some point between 1869 and 1872, someone— perhaps from Bancroft's staff—copied out sections of a five-part article which appeared in the Boston *Commercial Bulletin* in March and April of 1869, entitled "Some of the Early Men of the North-West Coast, by Webfoot." The copied Bancroft version, which does not appear to be in Phelps's hand, makes no textual changes from this published version, and the division into five numbered sections, corresponding exactly to the five-fold published division but otherwise having no logical justification, shows without a doubt its source. A few fairly substantial sections were omitted, however, where the account by "Webfoot" borrowed from another already-published source or reflected upon some of his own experiences which were not directly related to the Northwest. In the format presented below, such omitted sections have been restored and marked by brackets.

Captain Phelps, otherwise known as "Webfoot," was merely following a popular 19th-century literary custom in choosing a pseudonym. There is no question that he was Webfoot. This is demonstrated by his letter to Bancroft and in other sources. Some of Phelps's additional papers, still preserved by his family, include notes and clippings which show that he published both "Solid Men" and his memoirs, entitled *Fore & Aft; or, Leaves from the Life of an Old Sailor*, by Webfoot, in serial form in the *Commercial Bulletin*, the latter, at least in part, in 1868. In 1871 Phelps paid for the commercial printing of *Fore & Aft* in book form, thus making available to posterity an entertaining and valuable account of a seafaring life.[7] In the case of "Some of the Early Men," however, had no copy been made by Bancroft's history collectors, its valuable contents would very probably not have been used by Morison and the others.

In his publications Phelps emerges as a literate and interested man. These traits are displayed as well in his other written records. On his longer voyages, at least, Phelps was in the habit of keeping detailed journals, intended for the entertainment of his wife Lusanna. Phelps's main long-duration voyages were in the California trade, and there he remained in communication, however tenuous, with New England. Lusanna wrote him numerous letters in care of any California-bound vessel, and of these there were a goodly number even in pre-gold rush days. Phelps returned sections of his journal by the same means. "I am most amused with your Journal hope you are still journalizing as your pen ever gratifies me," she wrote in October 1841 in a letter which he received seven months later in Monterey. Two of Captain Phelps's journals on the California coast have been published, and they add useful information to pre-annexation history.[8] The total collection of Phelps's writings, published and unpublished, is thus overall quite substantial, and fully sufficient to provide a portrait of an adventurous and highly-regarded man.

Phelps was born in Gloucester, Massachusetts, in 1802, the son of a well-established apothecary, postmaster, and magistrate in that town. At the tender but not unusual age of

---

[7]Boston: Nichols & Hall, 1871.

[8]*Alta California 1840-1842* (1987), and *Frémont's Private Navy: the 1846 Journal of ...* (1987); both volumes edited by Briton C. Busch.

fourteen, Phelps went to sea as a cabin-boy, thus disappointing a father who wished his son to follow his own steps to Harvard University. Phelps was to give up the sea only upon retirement, but his family background no doubt helped make him both a reader and a writer. His early career was varied and exciting, and included sealing in the Indian Ocean, coasting out of Cape Town, and serving aboard a British sloop-of-war and again in the Chilean Navy during a short war against Peru. Between 1823 and 1831, Phelps led a more regular life in trading voyages to the Mediterranean, Europe, and the Caribbean. In 1831, after fifteen years at sea, he had worked his way up to master of the Boston trading brig *Mermaid,* sailing to the Barbary coast for wool and to Smyrna for tobacco and other Turkish products. All went well in this and similar voyages until Phelps was wrecked near Plymouth in a fierce winter gale in 1836, his vessel, the brig *Regulator,* a complete loss, half his crew drowned, and the remainder, including Phelps, suffering badly from frostbite.

Although Phelps did not give up his profession after this disaster, he did purchase property in Lexington, on the outskirts of Boston, probably because his second wife (his first wife, of whom little is known, died in 1831), Lusanna Tucker Bryant, hailed from there. Three children followed in 1836, 1838, and 1845, but Phelps had meanwhile turned to the California trade, having been offered the command of the Bryant, Sturgis & Company's ship *Alert.* The *Alert's* voyage of 1840-2 is discussed in detail in Phelps's journal of that voyage, now published, and the editor's introduction outlines the nature of the hide and tallow trade in which Phelps was involved. That trade was made famous through the classic account of Richard Henry Dana, *Two Years Before the Mast.* Phelps's account differs from Dana's in that Phelps was as a ship's captain much better placed to see more of California and its inhabitants—and less of the hard work involved in filling a ship's hold with hides, for Dana sailed before the mast.

Phelps sailed for home in 1843, only to leave once again for California in 1845, this time as master and supercargo for the bark *Moscow*, owned by Joseph B. Eaton. No sooner was Phelps in California than he found himself involved in the sudden acquisition of California by the United States, which adventure is recounted in some detail in *Fore & Aft* and in *Frémont's Private Navy*, his 1846 journal. Though exciting enough, no doubt, this was not a time to expect substantial profits from the dry goods trade. Lusanna's letters make clear that at least the family at home was not feeling particularly well-off: "Our house begins to look shabby and it ought to be shingled. If I get money enough from you I shall do it as it leaks badly...I find my expenses are double to what they were when you was away before. Our children are larger and a third one makes a great difference. I study economy every way I can," she wrote in the winter of 1847, adding however that Eaton, the vessel's owner, was most considerate and helpful.[9] The *Moscow* proved a bad bargain, however, since she was condemned as unseaworthy at San Diego about the time Lusanna penned these words. Phelps eventually reached home in 1849 in a schooner from Panama, and for a while he retired from the sea. After five years on his snug little farm, however, the urge to sail again proved irresistible, and Phelps was outward bound for California and Canton aboard the medium clipper *Arcadia*. He soon found that California had lost all appeal; much had changed between 1849 and 1855. After reaching New York in 1856, he took off his sea boots, and retired from the sea for good.

In his later years, Phelps proved to have made some wise investments, and he emerged as a community leader in Lexington, involved in banking and other commercial matters. Before he died in 1875, his pen, as has been seen, remained active, with publication of both "Fore & Aft" and "Solid Men" along with numerous shorter pieces in newspaper for-

---

[9]Lusanna Phelps to William D. Phelps, 8 January 1847, Phelps family collection.

mat, and the subsidized book form of *Fore & Aft* in 1871. Clearly he had kept in contact with his peers in the seafaring profession, for otherwise he could not have obtained the journals of the Boston men which he quotes in his account of their activities. Particularly important was the memoir of William A. Gale, a close friend of Phelps's and who had been Nathan Winship's clerk. Unfortunately, such journals have not survived, or at least have not come to light. They certainly are not to be found in any part of the Phelps collection, or logbooks, journals, accounts, and correspondence presented to Harvard University in 1927 by Phelps's surviving daughter Alice and now in the Houghton Library. Nor do they exist in the small collection of letters, documents, and clippings still held by his family and intended for the same Houghton collection. As a result, the data gathered by Phelps in "Solid Men" hold unique value as a source for the history of these pioneers in the Northwest.

It is fitting that William Sturgis's own account of the Northwest trade, first presented as a lecture which was printed in *Hunt's Merchants' Magazine* in 1846,[10] is reprinted below, as Appendix I. Sturgis was well-known to Phelps as a fellow member of the Boston world of commerce, trade, and seafaring and as part-owner of some of the vessels which Phelps commanded. But there is another connection here of note. Phelps was working in a tradition first set down by Sturgis, some of whose early historical remarks were available to Phelps.

Sturgis ranks as particularly important in the history of the Boston maritime fur trade, for he himself had made four voyages in it and probably helped Phelps come to his own assessments of the trade. Born in Barnstable, Massachusetts, in 1782, he was a ship-master's son. He entered the service of

---

[10]*Hunt's Merchant's Magazine,* 14 (1846): 532-38; also Howay, ed., "William Sturgis: The Northwest Fur Trade." Sturgis's journal is published as Jackman, ed., *The Journal of William Sturgis* (1978).

James and Thomas H. Perkins, who were prominent in the Pacific and China trades. As a green foremasthand he sailed to the Northwest Coast in the *Eliza,* went to China, and returned to Boston a third mate. The next year he made his second cruise, this time as first mate of the *Caroline,* owned by James and Thomas Lamb, and he returned home as her master. He later commanded the *Athualpa* of 209 tons and features heavily in Phelps's account of the trade. Sturgis retired after only twelve years at sea, and when he came ashore he did so a very wealthy man. He was elected to the Massachusetts Legislature in 1814, and was until 1845 almost continuously a member of the House or Senate. In 1846 he lectured on the subject of the history of the Northwest trade, and the secretary of a Boston literacy society, Elliot C. Cowdin, had the good sense to make a transcript of it and have it printed in *Hunt's Merchants' Magazine.*[11] This lecture appeared before Phelps's manuscript, and indeed predates it by at least a decade and perhaps as much as a generation. Sturgis died in 1863 after a venerable and worthy life in business and public works.

By no means were these traders such as Sturgis all from Boston, or even from Massachusetts. Morison's persuasive prose, the first eloquent testimony to the importance of the maritime fur trade in American history, misleads us into thinking that it was a Boston business. It was not, at least not totally. The *New Hazard* hailed from Salem, Massachusetts. John Jacob Astor's *Tonquin,* blown up in Vancouver Island waters in 1810, sailed out of New York. The *Snow Susan,* Captain William Trotter, called Providence, Rhode Island, home port. Most of the vessels, however, were from Boston: in 1790 all four of the American vessels in the trade were registered in that port, as were the ten vessels engaged in 1800. Nine of twelve present on the Northwest Coast in 1810 and eleven of fourteen trading there in 1820 hailed from Boston.

---

[11]Howay, "William Sturgis,": introduction.

Because of this it is not surprising that the native inhabitants of the Northwest Coast called all American traders "Boston Men." This set them sharply apart from "King George Men," or in the local Chinook jargon, *Kintshautshmen*. They were the Yankee traders, the purveyors of spirituous liquors, the importers of goods, and the seaborne merchant mariners who became, if but for a passing age, a mere forty years, masters of the Northwest maritime fur trade.

If ever a tougher breed of sea traders existed in modern human history it is doubtful. The "Solid Men of Boston," as Phelps terms them, conducted an annual voyage around the world. They doubled Cape Horn, reputedly the world's most hazardous passage, without the loss of a single ship.[12] They faced the unpredictable perils of the roaring forties. They risked the slaking thirsts of the doldrums. They persisted against the countless hazards of a fog-bound west coast of North America. Not least, they contended with the native lords of the Northwest Coast, who, as circumstances were to show, were no docile breed. Their ships were captained by some of the most hard-headed, heavy-handed officers, many of whom owned their own vessels. Families such as the Magees, the Winships and the Perkins sent forth their stoutest ships and their toughest sons in a line of work that was as laborious and hazardous as it was lucrative and exotic. They were sea traders untrammelled by government regulation. They embodied a spirit of free enterprise and harbored a suspicion of authority. Theirs was the law and theirs the profits. They hated interference. They were suspicious of foreigners. They were transients on a savage coast, and made no provisions under governmental regulations, unlike their

---

[12] "The passage around Cape Horn from the Eastward I positively assert," wrote Captain Porter of the United States frigate *Essex*, "is the most dangerous, most difficult, and attended with more hardships than that of the same distance in any other part of the world." Quoted, Morison, *Maritime History of Massachusetts*, p. 53.

English competitors, to regulate the trade, to establish a monopoly, or to licence ships. This was an open commerce where the free-spirited Bostonians had no limits to their needs, and no rivals to interfere with their business.

Phelps portrays this enterprise as a Boston epic. He begins his history with but passing mention to the rivals of other nations—the Russians and the English—and he mentions a few of the early voyages launched by merchants based in China and Bombay.[13] Patriotism shapes his history at this stage, and this is because his intended reading public was American. Consequently, he moves quickly to an examination of the pioneer American vessels fitted out for the Northwest Coast trade, the *Columbia* and the *Lady Washington*. The *Columbia*, more correctly the *Columbia Rediviva*, was a ship of 212 8/95 tons, 83'6" long and 24'2" beam. Built in Plymouth, Massachusetts, in 1787, she sailed from Boston 30 September 1787 in company with the sloop *Lady Washington* of 90 tons. Owned by a Boston merchant syndicate headed by Joseph Barrell and including Samuel Brown, the architect Charles Bulfinch, John Derby, Crowell Hatch, and John M. Pintard, the expedition was commanded by John Kendrick, master of the *Columbia*. Robert Gray was skipper of the *Lady Washington*. The purpose of this and subsequent such voyages was to exploit the maritime fur trade of the Northwest Coast, the pecuniary prospects of which had been made public by Captain James Cook's voyage. The *Columbia* reached Nootka Sound, Vancouver Island, on 17 September 1787. However, Gray undertook no aggressiveness in trading, leaving that to Kendrick with whom he exchanged ves-

---

[13]The Russians were the first in this business, and their trade to China with sea-otter pelts dates from as early as 1741, perhaps before. The trade directly to Canton, via Alaska, Hawaii and Kamchatka, began with the voyage of James Cook, R.N., 1776-1779; see Gough, "James Cook and the Origins of the Maritime Fur Trade," *The American Neptune*, 38 (1978): 217-24. For a more extended discussion, see Gough, *The Northwest Coast: British Navigation, Trade, and Discoveries to 1812* (1992).

sels. Gray steered for the Hawaiian Islands, China, and then
Boston, reached 9 August 1790. The *Columbia* became the
first vessel to carry the Stars and Stripes around the world.
She sailed again for the Northwest Coast on 28 September
1790, traded on "the Coast" and went into winter quarters at
Clayoquot Sound, Vancouver Island. In May 1792 Captain
Gray sailed her into the Great River of the West—which was
subsequently given the ship's name. She reached Boston with
a rich cargo of oriental goods on 29 July 1793.[14]

In the course of the *Columbia's* first Northwest Coast
cruise, as noted, Captain Kendrick had shifted to the *Lady
Washington*. He seems to have done this for several reasons.
Not the least of these was that she was the smaller of the two
vessels and thus handier and safer for navigation in unknown
and unsurveyed waters. An additional reason is that
Kendrick intended to winter on the coast, and was the first to
do so, and thereby undertake multiple trading seasons,
preparatory to sending pelts to Canton.

Kendrick was, as Phelps states, keen on establishing
alliances with the native peoples of the Northwest Coast. His
intention was to establish an arrangement with the head
chiefs of the many villages in and near Nootka and Clayoquot sounds, Vancouver Island, then the focus of the maritime trade in southern latitudes, and thus be able to repeat
the success of the initial trade. Phelps devotes considerable
space to these "Kendrick deeds," as they are referred to by
historians and lawyers. They have a long and significant history. They were witnessed, Kendrick says, by certain officers
and mates, and were sent to registries in Macao or perhaps
Canton, with copies supposedly being sent for filing in
Boston. No accredited copy has been located. However,
Robert Greenhow, Hall J. Kelley and Hubert Howe Bancroft, all in one way or another promoters of United States

---

[14]Sadly, this famous ship was "ript to pieces" in 1801. Howay, ed., *Voyages of the "Columbia,"* introduction.

designs for dominion in Oregon and the Northwest Coast, have given attention to them in their books.[15] Kendrick's descendants endeavoured to claim much real estate on the Northwest Coast in consequence of his deeds. For some years during the mid-nineteenth century Congressional committees taxed themselves evaluating the evidence, and concluded that the heirs had no case.[16] The United States non-intercourse acts, forbidding trading intercourse with the Indians without government sanction, would also make these deeds questionable.[17] In any event, this side of Phelps's story is far from dead, because today the Kendrick deeds are receiving mention, if only in passing, in one of the major aboriginal land claim cases proceeding in British Columbia courts, the Meares Island case. Allegedly, Kendrick had undertaken an arrangement with Chief Wikinanish and others of Meares Island and Clayoquot Sound, as did the British trader John Meares, after whom the fourteen-square-mile island is named. Meanwhile, as historians and others continue to examine these early records, the heirs of Wikinanish and others, represented in the Nuu-Chah-Nulth Tribal Council, have petitioned that they never have bargained away their aboriginal rights to the Crown or any other party. The court has injoined against the timber giant MacMillan Bloedel Limited which holds the tree-harvesting license.[18] Meanwhile, the great trees, many of them of primeval origin and some showing aboriginal use dating from long before Kendrick or Meares ever made an appearance and disturbed

[15]Robert Greenhow, *The History of Oregon and California and the Other Territories of the North-west Coast of North America* (3rd ed. rev.; New York: D. Appleton and Co., 1845), pp. 228-30; Hall J. Kelley, *Discoveries, Purchases of Land, etc. on the Northwest Coast...*(1838); Hubert Howe Bancroft, *History of the Northwest Coast* (2 vols., 1884), 1: 254 n.

[16]*U.S. House Report* 43, 26th Congress, 1st sess., 1841, and *Senate Report* 335, 32nd Congress, 1st sess., 1852.

[17]Francis Paul Prucha, *American Indian Policy in the Formative Years* (1962).

[18]*Moses Martin et al. v. Her Majesty The Queen et al.*, commonly referred to as the Meares Island Case (British Columbia Supreme Court, Vancouver Registry, Action No. C845934).

their way of life, continue to grow and mature. Incidentally, it may be noted here that the *Columbia's* voyage also resulted in the building of a winter quarters on Meares Island. This station's location has been positively identified on Lemmens Inlet, and its Boston-fired bricks and various artifacts are testaments to the links established between two margins of the same continent two centuries ago. Captain Gray's Fort Defiance, as it is called, is now a British Columbia heritage site.[19]

Here as elsewhere on the Coast, the natives were jealously protective of their resources. The Bostonians were intruders. Kendrick was probably not alone in issuing orders that the traders must be circumspect in all their relations with the natives, and to treat them with care and respect, and not to take anything from them except by fair compensation.[20] Those high-minded principles were not to be pursued in practice. As the trade between the men of the *Columbia* and the *Lady Washington* advanced with the Clayoquot at the village of Opitsat, Meares Island, so too did the armed power of the natives. The Bostonians grew nervous; they feared a reprisal for infractions against native customs and ways. A well-armed party was sent on a pre-emptive strike, to burn Opitsat, and the journal of young John Boit, then a third mate, clearly demonstrates the inhumanity of the sordid action.[21] This constituted but one of several violent encounters between Bostonians and natives in the trade, but they are not reported in Phelps's history. Phelps makes no comment on the captivity of blacksmith John Jewitt of the ship *Boston* by the Nootka in 1803 which became a Boston legend, well

---

[19]Morison, "The *Columbia's* Winter Quarters Located," 3-7. Mitchell, "The Investigation of Fort Defiance: Verifications of the Site," 3-20, and Mitchell and Knox, "The Investigation of Fort Defiance: A Report on Preliminary Excavations," 32-56.

[20]Kendrick's instructions to Captain Gray, in Morison, *Maritime History of Massachusetts*, p. 55.

[21]Howay, ed., *Voyages of the "Columbia"*, pp. 390-91. For Robert Haswell's version, see ibid., pp. 312-313.

known to every school child.[22] Nor does he refer to the savage dispute between Captain Kendrick and the Haida chief Koyah which was another celebrated encounter and became the subject for "The Ballad of the Bold Northwestman," a favorite in the forecastles of the vessels in that trade.[23] The episode is related in Haswell's second log, in Hoskins's manuscript, in Ingraham's *Hope* journal, in Boit's second log of the *Columbia,* and in Bartlett's manuscript journal. The location was Houston Stewart Channel (otherwise Barrell's Sound) in the Queen Charlotte Islands, and the date, the balladeer attests, was 16 June 1791. The Haida, trading on deck, had seized the keys to two arms chests. Kendrick immediately took action. He ordered officers and men to arms. They fired at the natives, killing sixty of them. They then went to a nearby village and forced the return of some stolen property. It was an act of revenge, but it fathered desperate legacies: Koyah was demeaned in the eyes of his people for having been placed in irons; accordingly, he swore revenge. The natives did not forget past wrongs, as Joseph Ingraham of the brigantine *Hope* wrote on 7 December 1791.[24] The balladeer appealed, in this quatrain,

> "I'd have you all take warning and always ready be,
> For to suppress these savages of Northwest America;
> For they are so desirous some vessel for to gain,
> That they will never leave off, till most of them are slain."

---

[22]As a captivity narrative this work is indeed a classic. One recent publication of it is *The Adventures and Sufferings of John R. Jewitt Captive of Maquinna, Annotated and Illustrated by Hilary Stewart* (Vancouver: Douglas & McIntyre, 1987). The tale affords the historical basis for a much-debated interpretation, James Houston, *Eagle Song: An Indian Saga Based on True Events* (Toronto: McClelland and Stewart; New York: Harcourt Brace Jovanovich, 1983).

[23]Howay, "The Ballad of the Bold Northwestmen: an Incident in the Life of Captain John Kendrick," *Washington Historical Quarterly,* 20: 1929, 114-23. See also, "A Ballad of the Northwest Fur Trade," *New England Quarterly,* 1 (January 1928): 71-79.

[24]The urbane Ingraham supplies extensive details, gathered from other mariners. See Mark Kaplanoff, ed., *Joseph Ingraham's Journal of the Brigantine "Hope" on a Voyage to the Northwest Coast of North America, 1790-92.* (Barre, Mass: Imprint Society, 1971), pp. 179-81.

As for Koyah, he never recovered his pride or his power, and driven to revenge to recover his prestige ended his life in several vain attempts to teach the Yankees a lesson in native power.[25] Kendrick's life ended in an Hawaiian harbour in 1794 when a gun accidentally was fired and terminated the life of one of Boston's most celebrated and contentious sea traders. Such episodes convinced ship owners to increase the size and readiness of their crews, to arm their vessels more heavily, and to equip them with anti-boarding nets.

Another famous Boston connection in the trade, the Winships, were the subject of Phelps's interest. Phelps knew this family personally and had access to the logs of several vessels, including those of the *O'Cain* and the *Albatross*. Mindful of the fact that the Winships were a successful Boston business family and horticulturalists (the cultivating of roses at their Brighton mansion being their passion in later years), he was of opinion, correctly no doubt, that they deserved to be recognized as among the early and most prominent Americans in the North Pacific, especially in Oregon. Captain Jonathan Winship, Jr., went first to the Northwest Coast in the *O'Cain* in 1803. Mr. Abiel Winship was part owner, and advised his younger brother as to what should be done to prosecute a successful voyage. Jonathan Winship, Jr., went to the Northwest Coast, to Canton, and back to Boston. In 1805 he braved another cruise in the *O'Cain*, this time as master, and with him sailed his brother Nathan as chief mate.

Phelps used the *O'Cain* journal to reconstruct the events of this voyage. From this voyage we obtain an appreciation of an interlocking web of relationships—of Boston ships and men, Hawaiian food and Kanaka labor, Russian commercial demands and opportunities, Aleut seaborne hunting skills, and, above all, the nexus of human relationships required to hunt the sea otter—before expeditions continued their

---

[25]Wilson Duff, "Koyah," *Dictionary of Canadian Biography*, 4: 419-20.

progress to Hawaii and the Marquesas, to Macao and Canton, and to Boston and New York.

The vessel *O'Cain* sailed first to Oahu, in the Hawaiian islands, a 173-day passage of 22,492 sea miles without touching land. Upon the ship's arrival the local king and queen visited the vessel, and from their party the *O'Cain* was able to lay in a large supply of hogs, vegetables and fruit. Hawaiians augmented the crew, as was customary, and she then steered for the Northwest Coast, in particular to New Archangel, or Sitka, in Russian America. In these northern waters the Americans learned the Russian tricks of garnering sea-otter pelts: sending about fifty Kodiak natives under direction of a Russian head hunter and three other Russians. Twelve women were to run a shore camp, the base of hunting. The hunting area was to be south of the usual grounds, in an area hitherto unexploited. The ship furnished all supplies, and the Russian hunters were to keep a certain portion of the hunt's proceeds. The Russians proved good business partners, and the only objection Captain Winship had was that the Russian managers at New Archangel would not break up the party until all had become drunk. Winship feared setting to sea for the hunt with an intoxicated crew. But eventually the Russians had the good grace to quit the ship and to return to shore, and the *O'Cain* sailed southwards from New Archangel. She had a very successful hunt, the details of which are specifically described by Phelps. The *O'Cain* worked the coast southwards towards the Queen Charlotte Islands and then the Farallone Islands off San Francisco Bay.

Off the California coast and islands the hunters found the sealing excellent. Winship decided to make another visit to New Archangel (via Hawaii) to get more hunters and more fish and whale oil—to feed the hunters. This was accomplished, and by this time the *O'Cain* had from seventy to eighty canoes carrying about 150 Kodiak hunters. This second hunting expedition invited the response of the hitherto sleeping Spanish authorities. They objected to the American incursion, and sent Indians from their missions to attack the Kodiak canoemen. They did not succeed. The *O'Cain* sailed to New Archangel, returned her Russian hands and native hunters, and sailed for Canton, there to sell her cargo for a handsome price.

This second voyage of Jonathan Winship, Jr., met with entire success, and led to another in the *O'Cain* in the following year, 1809. Moreover, Jonathan's brother Nathan also sailed for the Pacific, from Boston in July 1809, in command of the ship *Albatross*. These 1809 voyages are unique, and for a number of reasons. The project for the settlement was a Boston one—"planned, projected and gotten up," writes Phelps, "in the counting room of Abiel Winship." The company consisted of Abiel, and his two brothers, Benjamin P. Howes, and a few others. The Winships intended to establish a base on the banks of the Columbia River. This had never been attempted before, and ran all the risks attendant with crossing the Columbia's stormy bar. The object was to have a fortified agricultural base and from there to enlarge the coastal trade. Phelps skillfully reconstructs the efforts of the Winships. He does so by using as his historical materials the journal of William A. Gale, who was assistant to the captain of the *Albatross,* and various Winship instructions and other papers.

Phelps provides a very detailed record of the Columbia River colonizing experiment. In late May 1810 the *Albatross* sailed up the river carrying supplies and livestock for a settlement and came to anchor off an oak grove opposite present Oak Point, Washington. There her crew on 4 June broke the ground, planted a garden, and commenced work on a log house. The local natives, "would brook no competition."[26]

---

[26]Morison, *Maritime History of Massachusetts*, p. 58. See also, Bancroft, *Northwest Coast,* 2: 131-35.

Having few arms, no marines or warships, the Winships were obliged to retire in face of large native numbers.

Thus ended the first American attempt to establish a settlement and base on the Northwest Coast. It may be observed that this occurred just months before John Jacob Astor's famous *Tonquin* voyage, which resulted in the building of Astoria at the mouth of the river. Jonathan Winship, Jr., says Phelps, had "hoped to have planted a Garden of Eden on the shores of the Pacific, and make that wilderness to blossom like a rose." Instead he was obliged to cultivate his roses in Brighton, Massachusetts. But this event was to have a logical sequel: later Portland, Oregon, was to rise nearby and become the Rose City using slips from Winship's very own rose garden of Brighton. In addition, the significance of the Winships' settlement is that the Columbia River served as a cog in a larger wheel of commerce linking Boston and the Atlantic world with western North America including Alaska and the Hawaiian Islands, the Marquesas and the South Pacific, Canton and Asian waters, and South American ports. When the continental based trade of the Astorians linked with the maritime possibilities as announced by the Bostonians, a true recognition of the Columbia River as depot, artery and fulcrum was realized. It is no discredit to Phelps that he gave no attention to the Astorians, content as he was to record the considerable achievements of Boston men in the greater drama. Indeed, it is a bias of history that the Astor experiment has achieved its current preeminence. But that achievement has its literary genesis in Washington Irving's *Astoria* (1839).

From the Columbia, the *Albatross* now sailed for Hawaii en route to Canton. At Hawaii the ship took on a cargo of sandalwood, not the first ship to have done so, that honor belonging to Kendrick. As Phelps says "A new field of commerce was opened before them, which promised better results than the fur trade of the North West." This was true.

A contract was entered into with the Hawaiian King, Kamehameha. Only the state of war existing between the United States and Britain, beginning in 1812, prevented the successful prosecution of this new branch of commerce. The royal contract for sandalwood, given verbatim in "Solid Men of Boston in the Northwest," presented an opportunity for the Bostonians that they could not take up in time of war, and placed them in a disadvantageous situation in their relations with the Hawaiian monarchy. These arrangements were pursued by other Bostonians in other times.

Phelps offers no grand finale for his narrative and the reader may be left with the false impression that the text is incomplete. But Phelps had made his points, in particular describing the voyages of the *O'Cain* and the experiences of the Winships. He had linked Boston with the Northwest Coast, and with the Hawaiian Islands, Alaska and Alta California. He had not overstretched his historical materials but had, rather, presented a spare and sensible account of Bostonians on wider seas. It was not his intention to report on the violent and sordid aspects of cross-cultural encounters, and unlike William Sturgis, the first sailor-historian of the maritime fur trade, he chose not to ascribe blame to traders or to natives. Phelps remained content to chronicle the progressions and passages of ships and men, leaving moral assessments to others of such an inclination—and in the end that may have been the more judicious course.

What wonderful imprints the Boston mariners left on the sea. Throwing tea into the harbour was one famous act of history. But certainly another was shaping a course beyond the harbour lights destined for Neptune's line and Cape Horn. Twelve months ahead lay the profits only yielded when the ship returned to home port. And in the interim were new worlds to visit in the Pacific, both South and North, and calls at ports altogether different from Boston and quite various in themselves. To have lived in Boston while the memory of such voyages still burned brightly was an attraction that William Dane Phelps could not refuse. And with true historian's zeal he put pen to paper, and we are all the richer for it.

The editorial principles adopted for this publication are those of current standard practice. Minimum intervention of the text has been undertaken, save only when it has been necessary to correct the material in the Phelps narrative deleted from the Bancroft Library transcription (bracketed). Identifications and clarifications are made in footnotes. Abbreviated citations of sources are given in the footnotes, and full citations are given in the bibliography of works used in research for this edition which accompanies the text. The Bibliography will serve additionally as an up-to-date reference for students of the subject wishing additional sources. In particular, the reader will observe our reliance on Judge F.W. Howay's numerous works. Wherever possible Phelps's narrative has been checked against details as provided by Howay, and discrepancies are given in footnotes. In all editorial matters our main consideration has been to give the reader a useable and literate text. We hope William Dane Phelps, mariner and man of letters, would approve of its present presentation.

Solid Men of Boston
in the Northwest

By "Webfoot" [William Dane Phelps]

[In common with the whole human race, we are under infinite obligations to the men, who, by their persevering enterprise, skill, and daring spirit, led the way to a knowledge of the Western shores of our continent, the history of which has hitherto been permitted to remain unwritten, or has only been presented to public notice, in the form of pamphlet or newspaper articles.[1] In the absence of any connected history, it seems desirable that, for the benefit and assistance of the future historian, others should, from original documents, letters, journals, and personal narratives, gather up such fragments as may be met with, and place them on record, thus furnishing from pages of the world's history a few examples of true manhood, lofty purpose, and persevering effort of men who, whether in the pursuit of commerce or science, long ago made their mark, deep and lasting, on the history and fortunes of the American Continent. It is a natural and laudable desire of such a man to live in the recollections of those he loves and honors; to leave behind him a name, at the mention of which the bosom of friendship shall glow, and the eye of affection brighten; which shall be a legacy of honest

---

[1]As noted in the Introduction, Phelps's manuscript first appeared in the (Boston) *Commercial Bulletin*; part I was printed on 20 March 1869. The first paragraph, marked off in brackets, was not recopied in the manuscript version now found in the Bancroft Library, University of California.

pride to his family, and which it becomes them to transmit as living pictures of actual life to their children's children. The old prophecy of the course of the Star of Empire has gained strength in latter years, and seems approaching in an undeviating direction towards fulfillment. Perhaps it will linger long over the mighty Empire which is fast arising on the shores of the North Pacific, where the woodsman's axe is now ringing the death-knell of the Indian, and the shrill scream of the steam whistle shrieks his requiem. There are those now living who were active participants in many a scene of peril and harsh encounter with the savages of the North West Coast, early in the present century. There are those, also now living, past the meridian of life, who (judging from past progress and present promise) will live to see the time when our territory will be continuous, from the Gulf of California to Behring's Sea, populated by a progressive people, before whose energy and advancing civilization will forever pass away the yell of the savage Indian, and "the wolf's loud howl on Onolaski's shore."]

The fur trade, commenced by the Russians on the coast in 1776, was not much known to Americans previous to the War of the Revolution.[2] In 1785 the Brig *Harmon*, of sixty tons burthen, was fitted out in China by some English merchants, and made a successful voyage to the Coast and back to China.[3] This was followed by several small vessels from China and Bombay. In 1787 the first American vessels fitted out for the fur trade of the Northwest coast were the Ship *Columbia*, of two hundred and twenty tons, commanded by Captain John Kendrick, and the ship *Washington*, of 90 tons, Captain Robert Gray. These vessels sailed together from

---

[2]No mention is given here of the British origins of the trade. For discussion of this see Gough, *The Northwest Coast* (1992), pp. 56-95.

[3]The vessel was the *Sea Otter* (previously *Harmon*). See J. Hanna, "Journal of a Voyage from Macao towards King George's Sound," British Columbia Archives and Records Service, Victoria, AA 20.5, SeIH.

Boston, September 30th, 1787. Captain Kendrick was in charge of the expedition. They arrived safely on the coast and pursued the object of their voyage until the latter part of 1789, when it was agreed between the two captains that Captain Gray should proceed to Canton with the furs both vessels had collected, while Kendrick should remain on the coast in the sloop *Washington.* In accordance with this agreement Gray went to Canton, sold the furs, invested the proceeds in teas and arrived in Boston in August, 1790. This was the first time the Globe was circumnavigated by an American ship.[4]

Captain Kendrick remained on the coast with the *Washington,* and was successful in obtaining a very valuable cargo of furs, with which he proceeded to Canton. After the *Columbia* left the coast, Captain Kendrick discovered and passed through the Straits of "Juan de Fucca."[5] While at Nootka Sound, he purchased of Maquinna, Wacinash [Wikiranish], and other chiefs, a tract of territory, for which he paid in British manufactures a fair compensation. The deed was signed by these chiefs, as documents are signed by people who cannot write in any civilized country, marked and witnessed. The witnesses in this case were the officers and crew of the *Washington.* Mr. [Robert] Greenhow, in his memoir on California and Oregon, seems to doubt the validity of the transaction, but gives no reason for so doing, except his manner of mentioning that the deed was "marked" by the grantors, implying that they should have written their names.[6] This seems requiring too much of an untutored sav-

---

[4]The principal records for the voyages of the *Columbia* and *Washington* are conveniently collected in Howay, ed., *Voyages of the 'Columbia'...*(1990).

[5]Kendrick had, in fact, been pre-empted in this discovery by the English trader Charles William Barkley of the *Imperial Eagle* in July 1787 who recognized the entrance as the long lost Strait of Juan de Fuca. Kendrick never passed through the Strait, but the United States government as late as 1872 in the Canal de Haro arbitration maintained the veracity of Kendrick's passage.

[6]Robert Greenhow, *Memoir... on the Northwest Coast...*(1840), pp. 121-22. Greenhow was Translator and Librarian to the Department of State.

age, king or chief though he may be. In the "Old Colony Records" may be found similar conveyance of the aborigines to the early colonists, "marked" and witnessed, which have always stood good in law and equity.[7]

These documents, it is said, were taken to China, deposited in the British Consulate, and a copy transmitted to Washington. This could not have been the case, as there were no consulates in China at that time. The probability is, that they were deposited with the East India Company.[8]

Captain Kendrick wrote to his wife of this purchase, also of depositing the original title in Canton, and transmitting the duplicate to Washington. It was never seen by the family, and the letter in relation to it was unfortunately lost about twenty years ago by fire, in the burning of a building. Some thirty years since, the legal representatives of the owners of the *Columbia* and *Washington* applied to the United States Government for a confirmation of the title, and it was referred to a committee, of which Mr. Corwin, of Ohio, was chairman, but, as they were not the heirs of the purchaser, they could do nothing.[9] Mr. Corwin said, "the claim was a just one for the rightful heirs, but they had not appeared." That Captain Kendrick did buy land of the Chiefs at Nootka is substantiated also by the testimony of John Meares, who represented an English company and endeavoured to establish some claim there.[10] Greenhow says: "Maquinna and the other Chiefs insisted that they had never sold land to anyone but the American Captain Kendrick," and this was in 1789. Captain Kendrick purchased the *Washington* of the owners, altered her into a brig, and returned to the Sandwich Islands,

---

[7]The legality of these documents, "the Kendrick deeds," continues to interest students of native land claims. The search for the missing documents has been unsuccessful. Copies may be found in Kelley, *Discoveries, Purchases, Land, etc., on the North West Coast* (1838).

[8]They are thought by some to have been deposited at Macao, where the East India Company had one of several seasonal bases for its east Asian activities.

[9]U.S. *House Report* 43, 26th Congress, 1st Sess., 1841, and *Senate Report* 335, 32nd Congress, 1st Session, 1852.

[10]Meares, *Voyages ...to the Northwest Coast of America* (1790), p. 146.

where he was engaged in a sandalwood speculation, and lost his life at Kanakia Bay.[11] When dying, he called his mate into the cabin and put him in charge of the vessel, with instructions to proceed direct to the United States. The vessel left the islands, but was never heard from afterwards.

And thus were lost all of Captain Kendrick's effects, his journals, records of discovery, and his entire property, the accumulations of years of severe toil and hardships, and leaving his family destitute. Truly [this was] a sad fate for a patriotic and brave man, whose name should not be permitted to pass into oblivion. The character of Captain Kendrick, and the sad termination of his life is thus spoken of by Captain Amasa Delano, in his highly esteemed narrative of his voyage round the world, published in Boston, in 1817. He says in referring to the Sandwich Islands and the trade in sandalwood and the various adventurers, who visited them for the purpose of traffic:

> [Captain John Kendrick, of Boston, was the first American commander who visited the North-West Coast of America, and who opened that channel of commerce, and the sandalwood trade of these Islands to his country, died at this place (Owyhee) [Hawaii]. His death was occasioned by a salute that was fired by an English captain in honor of the birthday of Kendrick. One of the guns was through accident loaded with round and grape shot, which killed the Captain and two boys on his quarter deck. I think it no more than justice to say something to the memory of this American Captain. Captain Kendrick was the first American who traversed these distant regions, which were before but little known to the inhabitants of this part of the globe. He taught many of his countrymen the way to wealth and the method of navigating distant seas with ease and safety. I was intimately acquainted with him in Canton in the year 1791, and I knew his character as long as he lived.
>
> He was a man of extraordinary, good natural abilities, and was noted for his enterprising spirit, his good judgment and superior

---

[11] Kendrick actually died in Honolulu harbor. For biographical particulars, see Richard A. Pierce, "John Kendrick," *Dictionary of Canadian Biography*, 4: 410-12.

courage. As a seaman and navigator, he had but few equals. He was very benevolent, and possessed a heart filled with as tender feelings, as any man I ever knew, and was esteemed and beloved, by all who knew him. I wish to impress it strongly on the mind of every American, not to let his rare merits be forgotten, and to cast a veil over his faults, they being but few compared with his amiable qualities.][12]

Such is the testimony of one brave and honorable man toward another,—the more to be appreciated from the fact that they were competitors in business. It is hoped that the Kendrick representatives may yet find the document needed to establish their claim, and that Congress will eventually make suitable compensation for the distinguished services by which the whole country has benefited. There are proofs in the family that Captain Kendrick was one of the famous Boston Tea party in 1778, and that he was with the celebrated Captain Cook in his last voyage of discovery in 1776.[13] To Captain Robert Gray, of the ship *Columbia*, of Boston, belongs the honor of the discovery of the Columbia River.[14] This will remain an established fact, unless strong proof to the contrary should hereafter be produced, and of this there is but a small probability.

Thomas H. Perkins, Esq., of Boston, was in Canton in 1787, and in 1789 fitted out the brig *Hope*, Captain [Joseph] Ingraham, for the [Northwest] coast trade, and shortly after joined with Captain [James] Magee, in building the ship *Margaret* for the same business.[15] Both of the above vessels

---

[12]Amasa Delano, *A Narrative of Voyages and Travels*,(1817, 1970), p. 400. The original text differs in some respects from Phelps's quotation, but the substance of Delano's remarks has not been altered.

[13]It has not been demonstrated that Kendrick was in James Cook's expedition.

[14]This is misleading, for the Spaniard Bruno de Hezeta was there on 17 August 1775.

[15]Perkins was in Canton when the *Columbia* arrived with the first American cargo of sea otter pelts; there he met the first mate of the *Columbia*, Joseph Ingraham. Returning to Boston he outfitted the brig *Hope*. She sailed on 16 September 1790, only five weeks after the *Columbia* returned to Boston. Kaplanoff, ed., Joseph Ingraham's *Journal of the Brigantine HOPE* (1971). Magee's *Margaret* voyage was published in the *38th Annual Report of the Hawaiian Historical Society*.

made successful voyages to the [Northwest] coast and China. The names of Messrs. James and Thomas H. Perkins, Theodore Lyman, Esq., and James and Thomas Lamb, all of Boston, and the owners of the Kendrick expedition, will stand as the originators and most prominent merchants of the North West fur trade.[16]

The participation of Capt. William Sturgis in the above trade, and the estimation in which he was held at home and abroad, is well set forth in a "memoir" prepared by the late General Charles G. Loring, and published by the Massachusetts Historical Society in 1864, in which Mr. Loring says: "There happily remain memorials, highly valuable and interesting, which, for the sake of history and in justice of his memory, should be put in a permanent form."[17] It is hoped that justice may not long be delayed in the case. The writer had the honor of commanding the last ship fitted out by Bryant, Sturgis Co. for the Pacific, and, with many others, would write in the hope that whoever may have the documents referred to, will not withhold them from the public. Hon. Samuel Hooper, who was of the above firm, informed me that Captain Sturgis loaned his log books to some persons who went out to the Pacific, and, much to his regret, they were never returned. The coolness and intrepidity of Captain Sturgis were well exemplified in his masterly and desperate defence of his ship (the *Atahualpa*), when attacked in Macao Roads by a piratical fleet of sixteen Ladrone junks, under the command of a noted pirate chief.[18] The pirates were repulsed with great slaughter, and the ship, with $400,000 on board, reached Canton in safety. As a good illustration of his character for self reliance and prompt determination, I quote a pas-

---

[16]Principal among those in the *Columbia Rediviva* and *Lady Washington* concern was Joseph Barrell whose associates were Samuel Brown, Crowell Hatch, John Derby, and John M. Pintard.

[17]Loring, "Memoir of William Sturgis," 420-73.

[18]Other chapters of the violent history of this ship are recounted in Howay, *The ATAHUALPA*...(1978).

sage from his opinion respecting the claims of Russia and the threat to confiscate American ships.

> The American vessels employed in the N.W. trade are well armed, and amply furnished with the munitions of war. Separated from the civilized world, and cut off for a long time from all communications with it, they have been accustomed to rely on their own resources for protection and defense; and to consider and treat as enemies, all who attempt to intercept them in the prosecution of their lawful pursuits. To induce them to relinquish this commerce, persuasion will be unavailing, 'threats' will be disregarded and attempts at coercion will be promptly resisted, unless made by a force so superior, as to render resistance hopeless; in which event they will look with confidence to their government for redress and support.—*North American Review*, 1822, vol. 15.[19]

Messrs. Boardman and Pope, and others of Boston and New York, whose names are unknown, were the owners of fifteen vessels employed on the coast, trading for furs in the year 1800. In that year, 18,000 sea otter skins were obtained.

Ships now were fitted out for the purpose of hunting and trading. The direct trade between the American coast and China remained almost wholly in the hands of citizens of the United States until the breaking out of the war with England. Thus Russian vessels were not admitted into Chinese ports, and the British were restrained from engaging in the trade, by the opposition of their East India Company; consequently, a large portion of the furs were obtained from the Russians, who were glad, to exchange their peltries for European manufacturers, ammunition, sugar, spirits, wines, &c.

THE WINSHIPS

Of the many thousands who have in past years visited the delightful gardens and mansions of the above gentlemen at

---

[19]The full citation for Sturgis is in the bibliography. This was an analysis of President James Monroe's message to Congress of 17 April 1822, U.S. 17th Congress, 1st Session, *House Ex. Doc.*, 112 (No. 570).

Brighton [Massachusetts], and have enjoyed the polite attention and kind hospitality of the proprietors, how few are aware of the fact that these celebrated horticulturists were long engaged in the North-West fur trade; that they commanded ships themselves, and performed successful voyages between the savage coast and China; or that these quiet and retired gentlemen were the pioneers of civilization, who first planted corn and laid the first foundation for a settlement, at the Columbia River. The only mention I have ever seen of this attempted settlement is in Greenhow's valuable work; but even in that the credit is ascribed to the wrong person.[20] As the writer is fortunately in possession of the Log Books of the ships *O'Cain*, *Albatross*, and other ships of those days, together with many letters and original documents in relation to the transactions of those voyages, it will be easy to show that the Winship brothers are among the early and most prominent men in the North Pacific.[21]

Captain Jonathan Winship, Jr. made his first voyage to the North-West coast and China, in the ship *O'Cain*, commanded by Captain Joseph O'Cain. Sailing from Boston January 23, 1803, Captain O'Cain had made a previous voyage to the coast, and was there in 1801. The ship *O'Cain*, of which Mr. Abiel Winship and Mr. Ben[jamin] P. Homer appear to have been the principal owners, was a first-class ship of that day. Mr. Abiel Winship, the older brother and merchant, writes a parting letter of advice and instruction to his brother, who is now embarking for the first time on a long and perilous voyage, informing him of the object of the voyage, and of

---

[20]Greenhow had written: "In that year [1810], an attempt was made by Captain Smith, the commander of the ship *Albatross*, from Boston, to found a post for trade with the Indians at a place called Oak Point, on the south bank of the Columbia, about forty miles from its mouth. For this purpose a house was built and a garden was laid out and planted there; but the site was badly chosen in all respects, and the scheme was abandoned before the close of the year." Greenhow, *The History of Oregon and California* (1845), p. 292.

[21]Here is one of Phelps's underlying themes: that the Winships of Boston were the American pioneers on the North Pacific, and that they had not been given their due. Too much credit, on the other hand, had been given to John Jacob Astor at their expense.

[the] course he wishes him to pursue. The composition of the letter indicates the writer to have been a sterling [that is, admirable] merchant of the old school, while the bold, open hand of the writing, and especially the signature mark him as one of the John Hancock class.[22] It does not appear in what station he went on this voyage, but probably as an assistant to the captain, as the merchant states that Jonathan owns an interest in the ship and cargo. Of this voyage no journal or diary is to be found, but from other documents it is shown to have had a successful termination. A valuable cargo of furs was taken to Canton, and the ship returned to Boston with teas, after an absence of over three years.

In October, 1805, Jonathan Winship, Jr.[23] sailed from Boston again as master of the *O'Cain* for the North-West, his brother Nathan[24] being his chief mate. Of the previous experience of these brothers at sea, nothing is known, excepting the voyage of the older above recorded—the supposition is that they had made some previous voyages. The *O'Cain* was now fitted out for trading and hunting. The journal of the voyage is before me, and as showing the method of pursuing such a voyage, it is extremely interesting. The ship's company consisted of about thirty, including officers. The ship was coppered, which was not common in those days, and, as shown by the Log, was a very fair sailer. [They crossed the Equator forty-six days from Boston. The old and ridiculous custom of being shaved by Neptune, to which all had to submit on their first crossing the Equatorial Line,—a custom long since obsolete,—was now duly observed. I copy the performance as recorded in the Log Book, that the sailor boys of the present day may see what indignities they have escaped by not being born earlier:

Nov. 13, 1805—on the Equator, in Long. 26° 38' West.—This

---

[22]Hancock was famous for (among other things) his very large signature.
[23]Jonathan Winship, Jr. (1780-1847).
[24]Nathan Winship (1778-1820).

day, between the hours of two and three P.M., the God of the
Ocean, Neptune, Columbine and Harlequin, came to pay us a for-
mal visit, and to shave all his sons that had not crossed his territory
previously. This custom, though a very ancient one, cannot in my
opinion be altogether approved of. The manner in which they proceed is to fasten all those who have not crossed the Line before,
down in the ship's hold. Then three of the crew, who have crossed
it, dress themselves in a manner to represent Neptune, who is the
God of the Sea, Columbine, his consort, and Harlequin, their ser-
vant. These three characters, dressed in a very ludicrous manner,
make their appearance on deck, and in the hearing of those below,
they hail the ship, and in reply to "whom comes there?" answer
"Neptune"; then, apparently to those below, Neptune comes on
board and takes possession with great formalities. He then calls his
victims up one by one and blindfolded. After asking them sundry
questions, he begins the operation by daubing their faces with tar
and filth of every description, then with a piece of iron hoop shaves
them, generally scraping considerable skin off their faces, and rins-
ing all off with a bucket of salt water. After this Neptune requires
each one to give a bond to pay him four dollars, he then salutes him
as his son, and gives him permission to cross his Line.

Another ancient custom was observed after the above,
which was established from a sense of duty, thankfulness and
religious principle, and of so pleasant a character that I must
transcribe it. There is in the relation of it an exhibition of
forethought and feeling of the Captain towards his crew, and
of the New England home feeling that does honor to human
nature. Such acts were productive of results that were doubtless beneficial to all on board, for during the entire voyage
there is no record of trouble with the crew, with which the
journals of many voyages abound. The journal seems to have
been kept by the Captain himself. He says:

This day, according to the general custom of Massachusetts, we
suppose, to be a day appointed for Thanksgiving Prayer and
Rejoicing, for which reason I ordered one of our best pigs to be
killed and a barrel of cranberries broached, of which was served out
to the crew a sufficiency for a good repast, to which was added double allowance of grog. For the cabin the steward had reserved a few

apples which were made into pies. After dinner we drank the established toast of "Absent Friends," to meet the good wishes of our
worthy friends in America. Thus passed the day all in good spirits,
with a determination to persevere and surmount every obstacle and
difficulty in our present enterprising expedition.]

II.[25]

[Again off Cape Horn, 25th Dec.

Killed a pig to keep Christmas with; this day a very singular
complaint is made by our people. Our large potatoes being principally consumed, the people are grumbling and complaining that
they cannot eat small ones. What makes this the more singular is
the consideration that we are eighty days out, and in a lattitude
where perhaps not one vessel in five hundred would allow the
sailors vegetables if they had them on board.

And here I would digress for a moment to mark a con-
trast. The writer, on his first voyage to the Pacific, was not
far from the same latitude at the same season of the year
where the above scenes occurred; and how was it in our
case? On crossing the Line the game of shaving was
attempted on us. The preparations had been making and
the thing spoken of for some days previous; but the candi-
dates for the barber's chair comprised three quarters of the
crew, and we determined not to submit to any outrage on
our persons, and we did not; but we were awfully shaved in
our stomachs. Thanksgiving and Christmas we were not
reminded of by any "best pig," accompanied with cranberry
sauce; we would not have grumbled at small potatoes or
anything else that would have filled the aching void, and
were glad to steal salt slush from the cook's barrel when an
opportunity offered to eat with our scant allowance of
bread. Here was the difference in the commanders, though

---

[25](Boston) *Commercial Bulletin*, 27 March 1869.

both of the North-West school: The one was of the Sturgis class—the other of that class spoken of by him, who, in the exercise of power, treated the natives with "wanton cruelty and unprovoked barbarity." Captain W. treated his men with parental kindness and studied their welfare; Captain E. was a tyrant, who gloried in the exercise of arbitrary power, who cared for nothing beyond the gratification of low desires, and whose crew would have blessed the sea that would wash him overboard.]

The *O'Cain* arrived at Woahoo [Oahu], Sandwich Islands, in a passage of 173 days, without a man on the sick list, having sailed by log, since leaving port, 22,492 miles, and without calling at any port for refreshments. On anchoring, the ship was visited by the King[26] and Queen[27] and others of the royal family, and was surrounded by the natives, who were anxious to sell hogs and vegetables, but were prohibited from trading by the Royal Savage, until he had disposed of his own stock, all of which Captain Winship was obliged to purchase at extravagant prices. After four day's stay at Woahoo, and laying in a large supply of hogs, vegetables and fruit, he departed for the N.W. coast. The crew was increased by the addition of a few Kanakas at the island. On arriving at the Russian settlement of New Archangel, in Norfolk Sound, Captain Winship thus records the feelings of a devout, manly heart. "We experience the extreme felicity of thanking the Almighty for protecting us in perfect safety, without meeting any accident since leaving our native country."

---

[26]Kamehameha (1758?-1819), first king of the Hawaiian Islands. A great warrior, leader, and imperialist, he acquired control of almost the entire island group by 1795. In 1810 he gained sovereignty over Kauai and Niihau, completing the geographical boundaries of the Hawaiian Kingdom. His rise to power is explained in Kuykendall, *The Hawaiian Kingdom*, Vol. I (1938). Phelps spelled his name "Tamaamaha" but "Kamehameha" is now the customary orthography.

[27]Possibly Kaahumanu, high chiefess, "Kamehameha's favorite among his twenty-one wives." Her significant career is briefly described in Daws, *Shoal of Time* (1968), pp. 55-60 and passim.

The Russian Governor (Barranoff)[28] extended a hearty welcome to one whom he hailed as a friend, and promised every assistance in his power. After several pleasant interchanges of dinners and social visits, saluting, &c., arrangements for trade and hunting were concluded. About fifty canoes were furnished by order of the Governor and over a hundred Kodiak Indians, who were all good otter hunters; these were in the particular charge and direction of a Russian, who was head hunter, and three other Russians. With the party were twelve women, who were to do camp duty on shore, where gangs should be left to hunt. The terms of service were only expressed by "a hunt to the South," the ship furnished every thing and the hunters to have a certain portion of the proceeds of the hunt.

The ship remained at New Archangel about a month, during all which time Captain Winship says that "the attentions and hospitality of the Governor and his officers were of the most agreeable kind. Presents of fish and game were daily sent to the ship, and every possible assistance was freely rendered." All this pleasant intercourse was not without some drawbacks, as the Russian idea of sociality is, to not break up a party until all the company are drunk. This seems to have occasioned much annoyance to the Captain, for he says (May 22nd, 1806, being ready for sea):

> Having a most excellent wind from the North, I did not consider it advisable to weigh anchor, as our visitors (the Governor and other dignitaries) being mostly in a state of intoxication, in number about fifty, creating such confusion and disorder among two hundred persons in the ship, that I concluded it would be imprudent to put to sea. At 5 P.M. our visitors had the goodness to depart, doubtless not one sober man among them. I saluted them with five guns

---

[28]Aleksandr Andreevich Baranov. The classic account of his work in Alaska remains Khlebnikov, *Baranov* (1973). Baranov, as is shown here, was successful in obtaining from Boston traders the necessary foodstuffs and other supplies to carry on the fur hunt. This early Russo-American commercial partnership was exceedingly successful and a material feature in the demise of British trade in sea otters.

and three cheers, and heartily rejoiced at their departure. The Governor, on landing at the fort, returned the salute with a like number of guns.

Among the provisions taken on board for the use of the hunters are mentioned 15,400 dried fish, 1,000 lbs. whale flesh, and a large quantity of whale oil. The last article is freely drunk by the Kodiaks and used for culinary purposes. And now the ship proceeded down South, the hunt begins. A musket was delivered to each hunter, with ammunition, flints, and all other equipments necessary, for which the head Russian is responsible. Under easy sail the ship jogs along during the day time near the shore, keeing a sharp lookout for otter, and laying off and on during the night. When a favorable-looking place is seen, more or less canoes are sent in; occasionally some sea otters were obtained, but the coast was very rough, and the Indians were numerous and appeared hostile. June 10th they anchored just north of Trinidad Bay,[29] and a party of eighteen were sent on shore to explore. They returned and reported that otter were abundant, and the existence of a sound, to which no entrance was discovered, after following the shore for two miles. Proceeding along the coast they anchored the following day in Trinidad Bay. The natives here were numerous and sold them some furs. The Russians were landed, and the canoes sent out to hunt. They also found here great quantities of fish. Two canoes were daily employed in fishing and kept the ship well supplied. The Indians daily increased so that it was necessary to land the field pieces to protect the camp.

The natives at one time increased to nearly two hundred about the encampment, and a strict watch was kept. The field-pieces loaded with grape were ready for an emergency,

---

[29]Trinidad Bay, in northern "Alta California" (modern Humboldt County), the site of a wooden cross erected by Capt. Heceta and Lt. Francisco de la Bodéga y Cuadro on Trinity Sunday, 1775; the Bay is generally regarded as the southernmost extremity of the "Northwest Coast" of North America.

and the trade was carried on by the Russians, who purchased a considerable number of otter—for those of the first quality not over fifty cents in value was paid for any one, and several were bought for two cents of beads each. The Sound spoken of was a discovery of Captain Winship's; it was partially explored and named by him "Washington Inlet."[30] It had two entrances from the sea, and the shores were thickly populated with Indians. Otter and seal were numerous.

The following day the chief officer of the ship and the Russian commander of the hunters, with fifty canoes, were dispatched to hunt and for a further exploration. Another party was sent to fish and was very successful, while those remaining at the ship effected a considerable trade with the natives, who came along side with sea otter and other furs. They also bought for sale strawberries and raspberries. On the 18th [June] the large party returned with poor results, having only 17 otter. The Indians followed, and exhibited so much hostility toward them, that no attempt was made to land, and Mr. Winship, being desirous to avoid a collision, prudently returned with the party to the ship.

During the remainder of their stay in the bay, tents for the purpose of trade were erected on shore, opposite the ship, under cover of her guns. The hunters also had their camp near the tents. The next day the natives made an attack on the shore party, but were repulsed by the Kodiaks, and one of the savages was killed. The ship remained here until the 22nd [June], when having filled their water casks, and laid in a good supply of fish, all of which was performed under the protection of a strong guard, it was considered better to abandon the good hunting ground there, than to remain and fight the natives, and probably occasion the loss of many lives. In such a conclusion Captain Winship manifested a regard for humanity and justice, not often exhibited by the N.W. traders. Pursuing their

---

[30]Unidentified.

course Southerly, they sighted the Farallone Islands off the Bay of San Francisco without stopping there; and arrived at the Island of Ceros, off the coast of Lower California, the 29th of June.[31] The next day forty canoes were sent out to hunt on the coast, and the balance of them were dispatched to hunt among the different islands for sea otter. Mr. Winship, the mate, with a party of Sandwich Islanders was left to kill fur seals on Ceros, while the ship was cruising among the parties, supplying them with provisions and water, and taking on board the proceeds of their hunt. The ship was most of the time at anchor in the Bay of Todos Santos, and port of St. Quentin [Quintin], where much trade was had with the Spanish Missions of St. Boyé and St. Domingo,[32] from the priests they bought many otter skins, and obtained bullocks, vegetables, and a variety of fruit. Leaving all the hunting parties well supplied, the ship returned to New Archangel, to procure more canoes and hunters. The three months hunt had produced furs worth about $60,000 in Canton. The passage back to the North is almost a dead beat to windward, therefore it was not much loss of time to call at the Sandwich Islands, which Captain Winship did, and obtained there an abundant supply of hogs, yams, potatoes and fruit. They sailed from Oahu for the North-West on the 12th of October, having on deck over a hundred large hogs, which were killed and salted at sea for ship's use. Calling at New Archangel, it was found that Governor Baranoff was at Kodiak Island, and thither the ship pro-

---

[31]Ceros, or Cerros, is now commonly spelled Cedros. On fur sealing on this and other islands off the California Coast, see Busch, *The War Against the Seals* (1985), pp. 16-20.

[32]Todos Santos Bay, approximately 50 miles south of the United States-Mexican frontier on the California coast, is well marked on any modern map. The bay of San Quentin (Bahia San Quintin) is another 100 miles further down the coast. Mision Santo Domingo de Guzman lay some 25 miles north and inland from San Quintin; established in 1775, it was abandoned in 1839. Mision de San Borja ("St. Boyé") was roughly 200 miles beyond San Quintin (founded 1762; abandoned 1818). Although several missions lay between Santo Domingo and San Borja, in this part of the Baja Peninsula the main track lay well inland without easy access to the western coast. See Weber, *The Missions & Missionaries of Baja California* (1968), pp. 34, 58.

ceeded, arriving there Nov. 7. Here they remained until Jan. 16, 1807. The weather during most of this time was extremely cold and stormy, so that it was with much difficulty the ship's work was carried on. Water froze in the ship's hold in the casks, and numbers of the crew were badly frosted when at work in the boats. Through the kind assistance of his friend, the Governor, Captain Winship accomplished his purpose and left for the South again, with all the canoes he wanted, and another party consisting of fifty Indian men, seven girls, two boys, and one Russian, and having on board a large stock of dried fish and whale oil to feed them with. Owing to a constant succession of adverse and strong gales, with bad seas, they were thirty days in reaching the latitude of 37°, when the Farallones were visited and a boat was sent out to explore the South Island.

The officer on his return reported a vast number of fur and hair seal. This is the first account of any ship's crew landing on these Islands, of which we have heard. The ship next stopped at San Pedro, in the Canal of Santa Barbara,[33] to procure bullocks and other provisions. Procuring from the Spaniards all that was needed, and a sufficiency of vegetables, the ship anchored next in the little harbor at the Island of Catalina, and the hunters with their canoes were sent off to seek for sea otter, around this and other islands. At this time there were forty or fifty California Indians living on Catalina, from whom quite a quantity of wheat and vegetables was purchased. March 16th—The ship being off Todos Santos, and becalmed six miles from the shore, twenty canoes were started off on a hunt to be absent three or four days. The following day (says Captain Winship) "we anchored at St. Quentin, where I went on shore to hunt for game, and returned on board with eighteen dozen curlews, eight dozen of which I shot at one time."

The *O'Cain* had now from seventy to eighty canoes, carry-

---

[33]The Santa Barbara Channel, which runs between the California coast and the Channel Islands, was generally called the "canal," following the Spanish usage.

ing about a hundred and fifty Kodiak Indian hunters, fitted out and hunting sea otter among the Islands of Guadalupe, Natividad, Ceros and Redondo, while other gangs were stationed on some of the islands to take fur seal. On this second hunt the business was pursued as before, only more extensively. The Spaniards, with a pretended jurisdiction, attempted to prohibit other nations from taking the fur-bearing animals on their coast; consequently, when the ship was at anchor in ports on the main, it was ostensibly for the purpose of trade with the Spaniards; and the canoe hunters were kept away from the ship, giving the appearance that they were not connected with her. The Spaniards would sometimes capture and confiscate a stray canoe with its contents, and the Indians of the missions would occasionally meet with the Kodiaks and have a scrimmage. A number of such are recorded, in which a few were killed and wounded on both sides; the fortune of war generally terminating in favor of the Kodiaks. The cost of maintaining so large a family did not bear very heavily on the ship, as the principal food for the hunters was to be found in great abundance, and to be had for the killing; the flesh of sea elephant and seal, with a plenty of fish and rancid oil, was "strong feed," (as Kane says) and they liked it.

The management of such a body of more than half savage men, to keep them under proper discipline, and profitably and safely employed, and at the same time to navigate a large ship and crew, and conduct the whole to a successful termination, was no small matter. It demanded persevering ability and constant vigilance of the commander, and he was equal to the occasion. Previous to the 9th of April the parties were all gathered in, the furs were embarked, and the canoes were taken on board. The ship on the above day sailed on her return to New Archangel, where the hunters, their canoes, and their women and children, and their appurtenances, were to be left. Captain Winship says: "We received on board one hundred and forty-nine Indian men, twelve women, one infant, and three Russians. These, with the ship's crew, constituted a company of over two hundred souls." Three days after two children were born on board. The passage North was long and stormy. The Kodiaks had their priest with them, and he often prayed for fair winds, but they came not, and they endeavored to beguile the time by exhibitions of their national dances and singing of the songs of their country, which helped to keep them good humored, while it delighted the crew.

The result of the second hunt is not definitely stated, but, from a memorandum which occurs in the Log Book, it appears to have been satisfactory. On approaching the N.W. coast, a severe S.W. gale brought the ship in dangerous proximity with a part of the Coast with which the Captain was unacquainted. The Indians recognized it at once, and assured the officers that there was a large and safe harbor under the lee. The weather looked threatening, and it was impossible to gain an offing. The Captain held a consultation with her officers, in consequence of which they bore away before the wind and rushed rapidly toward a rock-bound, storm beaten shore, of which they knew nothing, except from the representations of ignorant Indians. But the decision was acted upon; the ship was flying upon the wings of the wind to safety—or to utter destruction. It was too late now to haul off and reconsider the question; a single hour would decide it. The intense anxiety and fearful responsibility of that one hour none can know, but him in whom rests the sole charge "to guard the ship from foes or wreck."

The writer fully comprehends the feelings that pass like lightning through the mind of the master at such a time. There may be a harbor which these ignorant Indians have seen from the interior, but what do they know of the ship's draught? It may be a barred harbor, across which in such a gale as this, and blowing directly on shore, may extend a line of foam, to enter which would lead to swift destruction. It is a period when an hour of such intense thought and care may work in a man's life a change which years of tranquility could not restore. The ship rushes on, "the warning voice of the lee shore speaking in breakers," falls louder on the ear, the officer aloft shouts, "breakers all across the bow" the boldest holds his breath; again the look-out shouts, "one point overlaps another, there is blue unbroken water between!" and steering E.N.E for the blue line, (says Captain Winship) "we passed to starboard of a small island at the entrance, and thank God, at 8 P.M. anchored in a calm commodious bay. We had much occasion for thankfulness, for in our safe and quiet harbor, we could hear the storm howling outside during the entire night." This proved to be the eastern part of "All-Saints Bay," through which they passed in a few days, by Baranoff Straits, to the Russian settlement at [New] Archangel. Here they remained until October 9, when having repaired the ship, restowed the cargo, and settled with their hunters and the Russian authorities, the *O'Cain* sailed for Canton, via the Sandwich Islands. In their different visits to the Russian settlements, Captain Winship appears to have been in the most friendly relations with the Governor and all his officers, and frequently speaks of the kind services and constant hospitality received at their hands.[34]

The cargo on board, according to the Log Book and the supposed Canton valuation, would bring about $136,310.

Procuring at the Islands the usual refreshments, the voyage was continued to Canton, where they arrived in safety the last day of the year 1807. Sailing hence, Feb. 14, 1808, in company with the ships *Atahualpa*, Captain [William] Sturgis, and the *Augustus*, Captain Hill, they kept company for mutual protection down the China Seas, Captain Sturgis

---

[34]For accounts of American trade here and its importance to Russian activity, consult Tikhmenev, *A History of the Russian-American Company* (1978), and Bolkhovitinov, *The Beginnings of Russian-American Relations, 1775-1815* (1975), pp. 180-82.

wearing the Commodore's flag, until past the Straits of
Sunda, when they separated. The *O'Cain* arrived in Boston
the 15th of June.

The above voyage was no doubt a profitable one, as Captain Jonathan Winship returned to the Pacific with the
O'Cain early in the following year, and was joined by his
brother Nathan, who sailed from Boston in July 1809, in
command of the ship *Albatross*.

The First Attempt to Form a
Settlement at the Columbia River

was made by Captain Nathan Winship, of Boston. Greenhow, in his book on "California and Oregon," speaks of the
landing of a party of hunters at the river from the above ship
at that time, as though it were not from any well-considered
plan by a company of Boston merchants, but as a mere incident in the voyage of a trading ship. Mr. G[reenhow] also
states that "W[illiam] Smith" was the captain.[35] The credit of
the leadership in this undertaking is thus ascribed to the
wrong person.

The establishment of a settlement was a failure from
unforeseen and unavoidable circumstances but the attempt
was made.

III.[36]

A large building for a place of residence and trade, with the
capabilities of a strong fortification, was partly erected,
grounds were prepared for cultivation, and seed sown. It was
the first building and planting by any white men on the banks
of the Columbia; and adding, as it does, to the fact that the
early development of the trade of the Northwest Coast and

---

[35]Greenhow, *History of Oregon*, p. 292; for the text of Greenhow on this see above, n. 20.
[36]Part III appeared in the (Boston) *Commercial Bulletin* of 3 April 1869.

California was principally due to the enterprise and energy of Boston merchants and seamen, it should be truthfully recorded. To substantiate the above facts, I have before me the entire journal of the voyage of Captain Winship, from the commencement in July, 1809, to October 1812, terminating at the Sandwich Islands, where he was blockaded by the British during the period of the war with England. The journal was kept by William A. Gale, who was assistant to the Captain (and who was afterwards the pioneer of the California trade from Boston.)[37] The journal is written in a beautiful hand, in which all the transactions of the voyage are recorded, with a minuteness of detail that is very creditable to the writer. The list of crew shows that William Smith was chief mate, and the crew consisted of twenty-two persons.

The *Albatross* was probably a good ship of her day, but she was not coppered, and as her log only exhibits eight knots per hour, under the most favorable circumstances of wind and weather, with all possible sail set and with a clean bottom, it would be natural to anticipate for her a long passage. The expedition on which she was bound, having as one of its principal objects the formation of a permanent settlement at the Columbia River, was planned, projected and gotten up in the counting-room of Abiel Winship, Esquire, in Boston. The company consisted of himself and his two brothers, the Captains, Mr. Benjamin P. Howes, and perhaps one or two others. (General John S. Tyler, who is an active business man of the present day, was then bookkeeper to Mr. Winship.) Every article necessary for their purpose was provided in

---

[37]William Alden Gale was Nathan Winship's clerk aboard the *Albatross*. Winship later made a number of trips to California in pursuit of the fur trade. In 1822-23 Gale returned as supercargo of the *Sachem*, a pioneer in the Boston California hide trade. In the late 1820s he married Marceline Estudillo, returning with her to Boston. In the 1830s he was active on the California coast as agent for Bryant & Sturgis (1832-5), a major participant in the hide trade. Gale was a popular agent and trader, known locally as "Quatro Ojos," four-eyes, on account of his spectacles. He died in Boston in 1841. Bancroft, *History of California*, vol. III (1886, 1966), pp. 750-51.

Boston, except timber, and that they knew abounded on the banks of the river. On sailing, Captain Winship was furnished with ample and well-considered instructions and advice, (a copy of which I have). He is advised to select a site thirty miles up the river and purchase the land of the natives; build a large two story house, in the second story of which all the cannon, muskets, and ammunition should be placed with port-holes in the side, and holes for musketry in the floor. The entrance to the second floor should be by a single trap-door, the ladder to be hauled up after the people ascend; and in nowise should a native be allowed on that floor. It is also enjoined to clear up and cultivate a piece of land, under the protection of the guns, and never have less than half of the men on guard; the object of trade being to procure the skins of sea otter, beaver, mink, fox, bear, sable, muskrats, and, in fact, any production suitable for the China or American market, and for which fair trade should be made, &c.

And now let us follow this old-fashioned ship, with her old-fashioned rig, many parts of which are unknown to sailors of the present day, with her uncoppered bottom,[38] in which but few sailors of the present generation would be willing to risk a voyage round Cape Horn. There are better ships now-a days, but no better seamen. In clipper ships, of late years, many cases of scurvy among the crews have occurred in a passage of less than five months. The *Albatross* called at Easter Island, her first stopping place, two hundred days out, with not a person on the sick list. In fact the word scurvy does not appear on the journals of either of the ships of the expedition, during their entire voyages, which fact speaks forcibly of the humanity, care and attention to the health and comfort of their crews, by the two commanders. The ship moved so slowly through the water, that grass had ample

---

[38]Morison notes that the owners of the *Albatross* neglected the precaution of coppering the vessel, and she took almost six months to round Cape Horn, with a reduced speed of two knots an hour. Morison, *The Maritime History of Massachusetts* (1921), p. 53.

time to grow on her bare planks to such an extent that when she had made westing enough to bear away to the north, around the Cape she was 162 days out, and her rate of sailing reduced two knots an hour, in consequence of the grass crop. The passage of Cape Horn was effected after severe toil and hardship, encountering a succession of heavy gales, mountainous seas, hail, snow, and icebergs, but all was bravely weathered, and without accident of any kind she arrived at Easter Island.

Mr. Gale's account of this island and its inhabitants is so graphic and interesting that I give it, verbatim:

> The island is situated in Lat. 27° 9' S. and Long. 109° 116' West. Owing to the cunning and thievish disposition of the natives, which is truly astonishing, we did not think it prudent to land, as it might have given rise to a misunderstanding. The captain went in with a boat and six men to Cook's Bay, and the ship lay off. While we were trading with the natives at a short distance from the shore in the boat, they swam off to us with potatoes, sugar cane, bananas, &c., for which we exchanged small bits of old iron hoops, fish hooks and nails, the last of which they seemed to set great story by. Beads and small looking-glasses, &c., they would not purchase, although they would steal the most trifling article they could lay their hands upon. Numbers would swim to us, and after disposing of what they bought, would wait till others came off & then divide what the newcomers brought among them all for the purpose of each one procuring an additional fish hook or piece of hoop. They would bring their potatoes in bunches lightly tied together, and, as soon as they had obtained what they wanted for them, would, as if by accident, while handling them to us, let them drop into the water, and immediately diving down, would bring them up for a second sale, and even went so far as to purloin the same things that they had just before sold to us, out of the boat, for the same purpose. They also made several attempts to steal the rudder of the boat, and so far succeeded as to break the irons by which it was hung, when we were obliged to take it on board to prevent their making off with it.
>
> Those who swam off to the boat, both men and women, had nothing on except a plat of grass or a small piece of Tappa (cloth)

round their waists, though numbers who remained on shore had long pieces of the latter stuff thrown over their shoulders, which reached nearly to their feet.

The women were well formed and handsome featured. These came off more for the purpose of attracting our attention, so as to give the men a better opportunity of exercising their thievish talents, than they did to trade. They seemed desirous that we should land, but when they found it was not our intention to do so, those on shore began pelting us with stones; a musket, however, barely pointed at them or discharged over their heads, the power of which they seemed to understand very well, soon brought them to reason. We saw whom we supposed to be chiefs, as they were tattooed a great deal more than the others, which only served to mark them out to us as the greatest rogues.

The women were likewise tattooed in different parts, and had the outer edge of their ears slit, which was made to hang down below the natural part as an ornament. We saw no kind of weapon among them, or any canoes. Amongst other things which they brought off to sell, were some small figures rudely carved in wood, and three large pieces of fish netting, which, although little or no value to us, must have cost them a great deal of labor, yet they sold them for a single fish hook each.

Occasionally they would bring off a bunch of potatoes tied up in grass, among which they would place stones, to make the bunch bulky. A pistol ball was fired through a small piece of board and given to a native. Immediately on his getting on shore with it, he was surrounded by a crowd, each one endeavoring to possess it. They seemed to be unwilling to trust each other for a moment, and being such great rogues themselves, they evidently mistrusted us; for this reason or fear, not one of them could be induced to come on board the ship. In fact, taking their wild situation in view, the little opportunity they must have had of getting any kind of information, situated in this wild part of the world, their cunning and roguery must have originated among themselves. They are in a state of anarchy, and every one apparently upon an equality.

But few of the natives appeared to be aged; on the contrary most of them were in the prime of life, and appeared to be cheerful to a degree. The men were far from being jealous of the women, and the latter appeared much chagrined at our declining to purchase favor, which was freely offered, and that they could not prevail on us to land.

A few of their words are similar to those of the Sandwich Islands, though the number is very small. This we were able to ascertain by having two of the natives of those islands with us.

Feb. 23rd, 1810, they anchored at Nouheavea [Nuku Hiva], in the Marquesas,[39] where they were visited by many natives, who with their chiefs, after making many professions of friendship and offers of assistance, returned to the shore. Wood and water were easily obtained here, also hogs, vegetables and fruit. Ten natives were hired to dive and scrape the barnacles off the ship's bottom, and they effected it tolerably well. After a long run of nearly eight months the bottom had become very foul; some of the barnacles which came off were four inches in length. On the 28th the ship was ready for sea; every day the natives in their canoes visited the ship in large numbers, bringing great quantities of pigs, coca nuts, bread fruit and sugar cane, which they bartered for bits of iron, iron hoop and other trifles.

Captain Winship also purchased a large quantity of red and white feathers of the tropical birds for the Northwest Coast trade. Being ready to sail it was found that one of the crew had swam ashore during watch and deserted. It had been intimated to the Captain the day previous that some of the crew intended to desert and remain at the island, and he notified the Chiefs that should this occur and they should countenance the procedure, force would be used to regain them; but all precautions were ineffectual. Dick had ingratiated himself with a Chief of one of the valleys, and it was found he enticed him away, and was now harboring him. All efforts to induce the Chief to give the man up were unavailing. Therefore two natives who were on deck were seized and put under guard, and a few four pound shot were discharged

---

[39]The Marquesas were first visited by Boston traders in 1791 when the *Hope*, Joseph Ingraham master, called there on the advice of Thomas H. Perkins who warned that Hawaiians had recently captured two vessels and that the Marquesas would be safer. Thus began a notable American-Marquesan relationship assessed in Dening, *Islands and Beaches* (1980), p. 22.

into the valley. This not proving effective, at 10 A.M. the long boat was manned with ten hands, armed with muskets, and dispatched on shore to seize some of the canoes. On the boats reaching the shore a skirmish ensued with the natives, who were armed with slings, spears, and clubs. Two were wounded, and unfortunately one of the natives was killed. Two of their canoes were launched and brought alongside. The Chiefs, finding at last that the four- and six-pounders and muskets were not to be trifled with, for the redemption of their canoes, Dick was brought down to the beach. The long-boat was sent on shore and the fugitive was delivered to the 2nd officer; he was brought on board and placed in irons. The natives confined on board were immediately released and put on shore, after presenting them with a piece of iron, with which they were well satisfied. The canoes were given up, and thus everything was apparently settled in an amicable way. The next day some of the natives came off and renewed trading; they informed Captain Winship that the man who was reported as killed the previous day was yet alive, and requested permission to have him brought on board and have his wounds dressed. This was immediately given, and he was brought in a canoe; but the effusion of blood had been so great that he died shortly after his wounds were dressed. It appeared that this man was shot while in the act of "slinging a stone at the boat's crew." The deserter was one of two Sandwich Islanders whom they brought from Boston. Learning that the other one was also intending to desert he was put in irons until the ship should get to sea. They next visited Roberts Island [Eiao], where Captain Winship landed and found a deserted village of about twenty habitations, but not a native was to be seen. They obtained a quantity of bread fruit and coca nuts with which they returned to the ship. The boat was hoisted up and they bore away for the Sandwich Islands. Mr. Gale says:

We left this group of islands, having been fifteen days among

them; in which time we wooded, watered, and procured considerable refreshments, and purchased twelve or fifteen hundred of the
red and white feathers from the tails of tropical birds, paying for
them at the rate of about three inches of bar iron per hundred.

[The Marquesas Group

The journal describes these islands as follows:

The whole of these islands denominated the Marquesas being
so near together that the natives often make excursions from one to
the other in their canoes, are nine in number, viz.: La Dominica, St.
Pedro, St. Christiana, Hoods, Rious, Trevenen's, Sir Henry Martyn's, and the two called Roberts Islands.[40] They were first discovered by the brigantine *Hope*, of Boston, Captain Ingraham, in 1791,
who named them after some of the first patriots of America, such
as Washington, Hancock, &c. In the year 1792 they were seen by
Lieutenant Hergest in the *Dardalus* [*Daedalus*], an English Government vessel, who, without any justice or right, took the honor of
the discovery to himself, and gave the above names to them. The
French afterwards gave them the name of Marquesas, on account
of the beauty and grace of the women. The inhabitants of these
islands are handsome and well-proportioned, the men, in particular, are very stout and well made, they possess a great degree of
cheerfulness, and are, in general, a friendly set of people. The
islands are broken and mountainous, the soil fertile: bread-fruit,
cocoa-nuts, sugar-cane, &c., are produced here in abundance. We
got some sugar-cane at Neuheavea measuring eight inches and
five-eighths in circumference.

The natives would not sell us any of their large hogs; these,
according to Wilson's account, they keep for feasting when any of
them die. This Wilson was a white man, who came on board the
ship when they arrived at Neuheavea, and requested a passage to
another island, which was granted. His own account of himself was
this: He left the ship *Lucy*, of London, at this island about five years

---

[40]Modern-day geographers recognize thirteen islands in the Marquesas group of French
Polynesia. The main islands include Hiva Oa (La Dominica), Mohatani (St. Pedro), Tahu-
ata (St. Christiana), Fatu Huku (Hoods), Ua Huka (Riou or Rious), Ua Pou (Trevenen or
Trevenen's), Nuka Hiva (Sir Henry Martyn's), and Eiao (Roberts). "The two called
Roberts" is unclear, but Phelps perhaps means Eiao and the nearby smaller islet of Hatutaa.
See Motteler, *Pacific Island Names* (1986).

previously. He was tattooed and went naked, except a piece of 'tappa' round the middle, like the rest of the Indians: could speak their language perfectly, and was considered at a loss when speaking his native tongue. According to his own account, he was chief over 4,000 men; Wilson informed us that he had known eighty large hogs to have been slaughtered at the death of one person. Their governments are divided into valleys, each valley having its distinct chiefs. These often make war, the one upon the other, although on the same island and close to each other. All prisoners taken in battle are obliged to cast lots, when every other one is butchered, baked and eaten like a hog, by the conquering party; and of this I have no doubt, for while lying in the port of Anna Maria one of their warriors visited the ship in his canoe, having a human scalp on each of his ankles and wrists, and a skull bone fastened to his side; but, on our testifying the abhorrence we felt at such ornaments, he quickly returned to the shore, and we saw nothing more of the kind.

Their instruments of war are spears, clubs and slings. With the latter they can throw stones to a considerable distance and with great exactness. Most of the men were tattooed from the crown of their heads to the soles of their feet, not excepting even their very eyelids. The females, some of whom are of very light complexion, do not use this kind of ornament as much as the men do. The stuff which they prick into their skin is a dark blue, similar to India ink.]

With the bed of barnacles removed from the bottom of the ship and her sailing condition much improved, they bore away for the Sandwich Islands, where it was necessary to call to procure extra men and provisions, and where Captain Winship expected to find letters from his brother, which would determine his own movements. The Islands of Atooi [Kaua'i], Mowhee [Maui], Onuhow [Nihau], and others were visited, as no single one could furnish sufficient supplies. At Oahu the King, Tamaamaha, "Billy Pitt,"[41] his prime minister, and all the Royal Family, visited the ship. The natives were not allowed by his Majesty to trade until he had

[41]Kalanimoku, or Billy Pitt (d. 1827), was prime minister under Kamehameha I, II, and III; Kalanimoku was Hawaiian, and he took the name "Mr. Pitt" or "Billy Pitt" in admiration of the celebrated English statesman.

disposed of all the hogs and other produce which he had to sell. Letters and instructions were also found here from the Captain of the *O'Cain*, advising his brother "to proceed with all possible dispatch to the Columbia River, to anticipate any movement of the Russians in that direction, and recommending as the best location on the river a spot about thirty miles above Gray's Harbor,"[42] with ample and minute directions and advice regarding the construction and management of the settlement to be established there, and of their joint operations afterwards. The *Albatross* left the islands April 13th, bound to the Columbia River, with an addition to her crew of twenty-five natives. She arrived at and entered the river May 26th, and passing the Chinook Indian village,[43] anchored about three miles above. The five following days were employed in sounding the channel, the ship making very slow progress up the river, as the passage was found to be very intricate, and the current very strong; thus feeling their way day by day, the ship following the boats and often anchoring.

June 1, 1810, Captain Winship and Mr. Smith (the mate) set out in the whale-boat to search for a spot which would answer for the intended settlement, and returned at 7 P.M. having found a place about five miles above where they anchored which seemed well calculated for the purpose. Owing to unfavorable weather and strong currents, the ship did not reach there until the 4th.

And now, during their operations at this place, we will copy from the journal of Mr. Gale their doings each day:—

---

[42]Now Grays Harbor, discovered 7 May 1792 by Captain Robert Gray of the *Columbia Rediviva*. Joseph Whidbey, of Captain George Vancouver's expedition, named it Gray's Harbor to honor its discoverer. Gray called it Bullfinch Harbor in honor of one of his Boston ship's owners. Phillips, *Washington State Place Names*, p. 57.

[43]Now Chinook, Washington, named for the Tsinuk that occupied the lower banks of the Columbia River. Their strategic position enabled them to dominate the trade of the estuary, coast and river even prior to the arrival of white traders, and their language, augmented by French, English, and others, became the Chinook lingua-franca used by traders and pioneers. Phillips, *Washington State Place Names*, pp. 26-27.

June 4th—Came to with the best bower in four fathoms, within 15 or 20 yards of the bank where the settlement is to be established and carried a hawser from the bow and made fast to the trees on shore. Part of the crew employed in unbending the sails. The carpenter, with the rest of the hands, and all the Sandwich Islanders, on shore felling and hewing trees for timber for the house.

June 5th—All hands employed on board and on shore as yesterday. Captain Winship and the second officer superintending the work on shore, building the log house, felling and hewing young trees, and clearing and digging upon a spot of land to plant. (The first breaking of soil by a white man in Oregon.)

The 6th and 7th—All hands employed on shore as above. The ship's tailor at work making clothes for the party who were to be left at the settlement.

June 8th—Hands employed in felling trees. At night, heavy rains. The following morning the rain continuing, found that the river had risen so much that the lot of land appropriated for the settlement was covered with one to two feet of water, and at the house it was about eighteen inches in depth. This proved a very unlucky circumstance as the building of it had progressed considerably, being already raised in height ten feet with timber, and the spot of ground which had been cleared and dug up, in which was already planted the seeds of some vegetables, was in the course of the forenoon completely overflown. The whole will now have to be pulled to pieces and begun afresh if a more convenient place can be found. Mr. Smith, with the whale boat, was sent out to search for one.

June 9th—Mr. Smith returned to the ship, and it was determined by Captain Winship to pull to pieces that part of the house which had been put up and float the logs about a quarter of a mile further down stream on the same side, where the land is somewhat higher. In consequence of the above determination—the gang on shore consisting of twenty-eight men, were employed in drawing the logs to the water to float them down to the new place. Every day, since arriving in the river, the ship had been visited by the Indians in their canoes bringing a few furs and some salmon for trade; but they did not come in large numbers, and had not been troublesome.

IV.[44]

June 10th—The people employed as yesterday. This afternoon several canoes arrived from Chinook[45] and Cheheeles,[46] containing many natives all armed with bows and arrows or muskets; they informed us that the Calaworth[47] tribe, who had a village close to the place where we are building the house, had killed one of their chiefs about ten months since, and that they had now come up the river for the purpose of punishing them, and intended giving them battle on the morrow. At 4 o'clock the next morning the shore gang was sent on shore to work as usual, which they continued until 11 A.M., when, observing that the Indians, with their arms, began to gather where the people were at work, without any apparent design of attacking one another, it was strongly suspected that they were planning to cut off our people on shore, in which case, if they could have put it in practice, there would have been with the few hands remaining on board but a bare possibility of escaping with the ship. Some of the shore party were therefore immediately ordered on board, and the others were set to work opposite to the ship, getting some logs into the water. Here they were under cover of the guns, which from apprehension of trouble, had been loaded with grape and cannister. The Indians continued to muster on shore, yet declared that the quarrel was entirely among themselves, which we very much doubted, as they were all mixed together or wandering singly about, without fear of each other, which increased our suspicions. One thing is certain, the Chinooks are strongly set against our coming up the River, wishing, as they say, the house should be built among themselves and the lower tribes, and on another account, as they are in the habit of purchasing skins of the upper tribes and reselling them to the ships which occasionally arrive at the River, they are afraid and certainly with reason, that the settlement being established so far up, will tend to injure their own trade, and they are no doubt determined to prevent it if possible. Their

---

[44](Boston) *Commercial Bulletin*, 10 April 1869.

[45]This reference is to the Chinook (Tsinuk) village; the term is more widely used for those Indians occupying the lower Columbia River.

[46]Now spelled Chehalis, meaning "shining sands." The Chehalis native village was at the mouth of the river Chelais at Grays Harbor, Washington. Phillips, *Washington State Place Names*, p. 25.

[47]"Calaworth" is perhaps Kwalhioqua, a nearby Columbia River tribe.

interference serves only to prevent our work going on as we wish. They might easily be brought to reason by the use of force, but it would last no longer than while the ship was here, and when she left the river those left behind must suffer for it. Any force the ship could leave would not be sufficient to defend the house if the Indians should attack them, while to openly cultivate the ground would give the natives a chance to pick them off easily.

June 11th—Again the men were sent on shore to resume their work, which they continued for about two hours when the Indians gathering around them in considerable numbers, and being observed to send their women and children away, with other suspicious circumstances, the hands declared they did not feel safe to be on shore without arms. The officer therefore immediately came on board with them, and we soon after dropped the ship down opposite the new place, intending to go on with our work in the morning. While moving the ship the natives were scattered about among the trees, firing their muskets and shouting. One of the savages pointed a musket at Captain Winship while he was sitting on the taffrail, but did not fire. During the night we got the waist nettings up and loaded all the muskets, intending to give them a warm reception should they make an attempt on the ship. We sent the long boat on shore to clear away some bushes that lined the bank, but these rascals gathered round with hostile intent, and the party were called on board. Shortly after three Chiefs and some other natives came alongside, but the chiefs were not allowed on board. When he spoke to them concerning their conduct, all we could get in reply was, they were not afraid of us, but they wanted us to return down the river. Much to our chagrin we find it is impossible to prosecute the business as we intended, and we have concluded to pass farther down. On making this known to the Chinooks they appeared quite satisfied, and sold us some furs. It is intended, should it not be thought proper to leave the settlers here, if there should occur a chance, to punish these fellows for their insolence as it deserves.

June 12th—The ship dropped further down river, and it was now determined to abandon all attempts to force a settlement.

The disappointment must have been very aggravating to Captain Winship to be compelled to give up the cherished hope of an establishment to which so much thought, care and labor had been devoted. The course too often pursued by traders among the Indians[48] was not adopted by Captain Winship. A regard for the rights of others, and a strong sense of justice and humanity, guided his judgment in withdrawing peaceably. The country was theirs. They had an undisputed right to resist the attempts of any person, or persons who should endeavour to dispossess them of the country where God and Nature had planted them; and their right in the matter does not appear to have been contested. No mention of an offer to purchase is made—but Mr. Gale moralizes thus:—

> We have taken off the hogs and goats, which were put on shore for the use of the settlement, and thus we have to abandon the business, after having, with great difficulty and labor, got about forty-five miles above Cape Disappointment; and with great trouble began to clear the land and build a house a second time, after cutting timber enough to finish nearly one-half, and having two of our hands disabled in the work. It is indeed cutting to be obliged to knuckle to those whom you have not the least fear of, but whom, from motives of prudence, you are obliged to treat with forbearance. What can be more disagreeable than to sit at table with a number of these rascally Chiefs, who, while they supply their greedy mouths from your food with one hand, their blood boils within them to cut your throat with the other without the least provocation.

Thus commenced and thus ended the first attempted settlement at the Columbia. It failed, not because an establishment could not have been made and sustained by force—the ship protecting all with her guns until a reinforcement should arrive—but because the leader of the expedition would not avail of advantages[49] which were to be obtained only through injustice and the shedding of blood. The sails again were bent and the ship slowly groped her way towards the sea.

---

[48]That of coercion, by the use of firearms and, sometimes, by the taking of property and hostages.

[49]In the Bancroft Library ms. of "Solid Men," at this point in the text there is a blank, unnumbered page, on which is written, in a different hand (perhaps that of Capt. Phelps), "No mention made by me of holding the Chiefs prisoner &c July 8th + after."

June 17 they anchored at Gray's Bay,[50] when the Indian pilot who went up with the ship and performed the same service on her return, informed the Captain that the natives did mean to attempt the capture of the ship while she was up the river; he also told them enough of their present designs to put them on strict guard for the future. The Ship *Mercury*, of Boston, Captain [George Washington] Eayres [or Ayres], was also at Baker's Bay, from California, and bound North,[51] both ships remained here, trading with the natives and refitting. The weather was very boistrous most of the time, which retarded the work.

July 8th. Many canoes being alongside, and some of the Chiefs on board, and it having been previously determined upon by Captains Winship and Eayres, about 5 P.M. eight of them were seized and put in irons. This was done in hopes to procure the release of some Russians who had lately been cast away, and some of whom were still supposed to be prisoners amongst them, and for the purpose of punishing them for their conduct to us since our arrival in the river, as well as for murdering and robbing some Kodiaks belonging to the *Mercury*, when Captain Eayres was in the river a few months previous. We had the good fortune to seize and confine the chiefs without any one being hurt, excepting one of our men, who had one of his legs badly bruised by the recoil of a carronade, which was fired in the bustle by one of the people without orders, but no injury was done to the Indians, only they in the canoes were frightened from alongside the ships. The prisoners were immediately informed of the cause of their confinement, and they without hesitation despatched people to endeavor to purchase the remainder of the Russians, some of whom they stated had been starved to death, amongst them; they informed us that the tribes who held these men in captivity inhabited the country three or four days journey from the river.[52] From this to the 13th the chiefs remained

---

[50]"Gray's Harbor"; see above n. 42.

[51]This 145-ton Boston ship had a long, lively career on the Northwest Coast, in the Pacific and at China. She had been on the coast since 1806 as a legitimate trader but in 1813 the Spanish at Santa Barbara captured her for poaching fur seal and sea otter. "With retributive justice she was armed and used to protect the coast against smugglers and poachers." Howay, *A List of Vessels* ...(1973), p. 100.

[52]On captives and hostages, Russian and American on the coast and in this particular area about this time, consult Owens, ed. *The Wreck of the SR. NIKOLAI* (1985).

in confinement, many canoes were daily alongside trading, and the decks were carefully guarded. This day the natives brought off to the ship a boy of 17 years of age, who had been cast away in the Russian schooner _____,[53] off Cape Flattery, about 17 months ago, and had been a slave among them ever since. Captain Winship paid the chiefs their demand for getting him, which was twenty five blankets, besides small presents of tobacco, &c. "Comcomcia,"[54] the head chief of Chinook, informed us that there was some more of the Russians at the place where the schooner was lost, but the natives were too strong for him to attempt getting them, and he was readily believed, for he apparently did everything that was in his power to procure them for us. Finding that nothing further could be effected by detaining the chiefs, four of them were released from irons and suffered to depart from the ship. One of them was put on board the *Mercury*, Captain Eayres intending to take him North for the purpose of attempting the recovery of the other Russians, the other chiefs were released from irons, but detained on board our ship, to secure their good behavior until we should leave the river.

July 19th, the two ships sailed from the Columbia, the *Albatross* bound to the coast of Lower California. The ship put into Trinidad Bay, where some furs were bought of the natives, and two flat-bottomed canoes to be used by the sealing party. July 31st, came to anchor near the South Farallones. Found on the islands two gangs of sealers, one belonging to the ship *Isabella*,[55] Captain [William H.] Davis, of Boston, and the other to the ship *Mercury*, before mentioned. A party of seven persons was left here in charge of Mr. Gale to take fur seal, and the *Albatross* continued on down the coast. Calling at the Island of Santa Barbara they found but few fur seal on the island; but the sea otter were very numerous in the kelp, and playing about the shore.

---

[53] The schooner's name was left blank by Captain Phelps.

[54] Comcomly; more precisely, Comcomly Madsu, "Thunder." His powerful presence features in many early journals of the Columbia River. See, for example, Gough, ed. *The Journal of Alexander Henry the Younger, 1799-1814: II, The Saskatchewan and Columbia Rivers* (1992), *passim*.

[55] Details of the career of this 209-ton ship, active in the Northwest trade 1809-16, may be traced in Howay, *List of Vessels, passim*.

There are about thirty Indians on the island, but they had nothing to sell. Leaving another sealing gang at the Island of Ceros, the ship returned North, after a long passage arrived at Norfolk Sound the 22nd of October. Here it was found necessary to discharge the cargo and ballast, and haul the ship on shore, to again clean the barnacles off her bottom. After watering and provisioning the ship and making the necessary arrangements for sea otter hunting and sealing they left again for the Southern coast, with thirty canoes and about fifty Kodiak Indian hunters, Nov. 16.

At Drake's Bay, Nov. 29, they found the ships *O'Cain*, *Isabella*, and *Mercury*. Dec. 4th the ship being off the Farallones, they communicated with the party on the island and found they had obtained 30,000 fur seal skins since they had been left there five months since. The gang was increased by six Sandwich Islanders, and the ship bore away for St. Louis Obispo, to wood and water and procure beef of the Spaniards. A party of hunters, with their canoes and women, were left at the Island of Santa Barbara to take otter. During the three days they were left here the hunters took about sixty prime sea otter skins. The ship then proceeded to St. Quintin where she again joined the *O'Cain*. The hunters of this ship during her absence had taken 1,600 sea otter skins and were still doing well. It seems that the two Captains Winship pursued their business of hunting and trading on joint account, in different directions, and with gangs on various Islands, the ships moving between the points of observation, supplying their wants and collecting the proceeds of the parties. Many furs were also obtained from the Spanish Missions in Lower California.

Apr. 1, 1811, the *Albatross*, leaving the *O'Cain* to look after the business of the Lower Coast, returned North to the Farallones. The party left here previously had taken about four thousand fur seal, and had been over two months without provisions, except what the island afforded. The ship [took] off the skins, supplied the parties, and proceeded to Drake's Bay, where a few days after she was joined by the *O'Cain* and *Isabella,* on May 11th.

These three ships remained here together about a month, each having gangs at the Farallones; occasionally the boats were sent to communicate with the hunters and take supplies to them. During all this time nothing is said of the Bay of San Francisco, so near by, affording a safer harbor than Drake's Bay,] where wood and water, bullocks and vegetables, were all to be had at Sasilito [Sausilito], just within the Bay, and from which point the communication with the Islands was as easy as from Drake's Bay. The very name of the bay is not mentioned in the journals of the *O'Cain* or *Albatross,* consequently it could not have been entered by either of the ships or their boats. The Bay must have been known to them, as it is recorded that two American ships were in the bay in 1803, viz., the ships *Alexander,* Captain John Brown, and the *Aser,* Captain Thomas Raben.[56] The supposition is, that our American ships in trading and hunting on the coast, were doing what the Spaniards might consider a contraband business, and, therefore, to avoid a controversy with them, it was best to always have a plenty of sea room.

The following June the *Albatross* was picking up the parties of otter hunters and sealers on the lower coast, and gathering in the proceeds of their hunts for both ships—she left there the 11th of June, having first taken on board a longboat load of sea-elephant to feed the Kodiaks with on their passage to the Northward. Another thriving plantation of barnacles on the ship's bottom rendered her in a bad condition to beat about 1,800 miles to windward. She arrived at the Russian settlement at Norfolk Sound after a passage of about fifty days, where discharging the Kodiaks and their canoes they landed the most of their cargo and ballast, hauled

---

[56]On the *Alexander's* career, see Howay, *List of Vessels* ; the *Aser* and Captain Thomas Raben, on the other hand, are unidentified.

the ship on shore, gave her another scrape, and in about ten days were ready to put to sea again.

They now proceeded South for the last time. Stopping at "Kighganny"[57] to procure spars, timber and firewood, their next stopping place was at the Farallones, where they were to collect the seal skins, and proceed from thence to China. The *Albatross* left at "Kighganny" the brigs *New Hazard*, Captain [David] Nye, [Jr.], *Lydia*, Captain [James] Bennett, and the *Otter*, Captain [Samuel] Hill. Captains Porter and Blanchard were also here, both Boston captains. The names of their vessels are not given.[58] Of the seven or eight vessels trading on the coast at this time, all but one hailed from Boston. It is no wonder that the natives throughout the coast designated all American ships as "Boston Ships," and all Americans as "Boston men," for with very few exceptions no others had visited them.

Sept. 27, 1811—The ship anchored in ten fathoms under the lee of the South Farallone. The parties were all well, and had procured since the ship was last here (in December) 53,000 prime skins. They remained at anchor here until the 2nd of October. The skins were all taken on board, and all the people, except Mr. Brown, who, with seven Kanackers (or Sandwich Islanders)[59] remained for a further haul, and to be called for by the *O'Cain*. At 7 A.M. the ship got under way for the Sandwich Islands.

The ship had been on the coast about seventeen months, and now left there with a full cargo of furs, so full indeed, that her hemp cables had to be carried on deck, and some of the water casks broken up to make room to stow the cargo below. The following is "an account of all the different kinds of skins obtained for the *Albatross* to this date, Oct. 1, 1811."

---

[57]Kaigany, a Haida village on Dall Island, now part of the state of Alaska.

[58]Lemuel Porter, we now know, commanded the ship *Hamilton;* William Blanshard commanded the ship *Katherine* or *Catherine*. These vessels traded in company and by arrangement. Howay, *List of Vessels*, pp. 81-89, *passim*.   [59]Usually spelled Kanakas.

Number of Fur Seal Skins taken by Mr. Gale
and party in 1810   33,740
Do. 1811   21,153
Do. Mr. Brown and party   18,509
Amount taken from Farallones   73,402
The Islands of Lower California   1,124
Total amount of Prime Fur Seal Skins   74,526
Number of Prime Sea Otter Skins (ship's
share) taken by the Kodiaks   561 tails 581
Do. bought by the ship   70 "   58
Whole no. of Sea Otter Skins   631 " 639
248 Beaver Skins. 21 Raccoon Skins. 6 Wild Cat Skins.
153 Land Otter Skins. 4 Badger Skins. 5 Fox Skins.
58 Mink Skins. 8 Gray Squirrels. 1 Skunk Skin.
11 Musk [Muskrat] Skins. 137 Mole Skins.

Estimating the above at the average prices then current in Canton—sea otter at $40, seal $1.75, tails $1.50, and other furs, would make the amount of sales about $157,397, which would [be] likely to result in a very fair voyage. It would be very interesting could we see an invoice of the outward cargo, by which the furs were obtained, the cost of scrap iron, beads, cheap looking-glasses, nails, fish-hooks, &c.

To many persons who have heard stories of the "North-West voyages," mixed up with considerable romance, the foregoing details and abstracts of actual and reliable journals of two voyages will no doubt be interesting, as they also may be to the dwellers in San Francisco, who as they look upon the lonely, barren rocky islets which stands as sentinels just without their "Golden Gates," can hardly realize that very early in the present century such golden crops of furs were gathered there by the "Boston men."

The *Albatross*, about the 1st of November, arrived at Oahu. The King and Royal family came on board when the ship was entering the harbor. He very condescendingly passed the night, with all his retinue, on ship board, receiving a salute of five guns at his reception and the same on his departure. The ship was furnished with a great quantity of hogs, yams, and taro, for which they paid in barter. The barnacles were again hoed off the bottom; the ship was fitted and ready for sea in two weeks and was now waiting the arrival of the *O'Cain* from the coast. She arrived about the 20th and the *Isabella* a few days after. The latter ship, belonging to Messrs. Boardman and Pope, of Boston, was on a similar voyage, and it seems that the three Captains about this time entered into a partnership, and prosecuted their voyages accordingly. The three ships sailed from Oahu in company, Jan. 1, 1812, bound to Canton. The ships, in addition to their valuable furs, had each a considerable quantity of sandalwood.

The second day out it was found that much time would be lost by keeping company with the *Albatross,* she being a dull sailor. It was thought expedient to leave her astern, and for the other ships to make the best of their way without her. The course across the North Pacific to the coast of China, lies mostly between the Tropics, where light winds and smooth water prevail, consequently it was very favorable for the cultivation of a fresh crop of barnacles in the *Albatross's* plantation, as the ship dragged her way slowly on the long route.

Arriving at Macao after a passage of 52 days, and at Whampoa the 26th of February [1812], they found their consorts in port. From this time to the 20th of April the ships remained in the river fitting, it being decided to return to the North Pacific again. The ballast and stores were landed from the *Albatross,* and she was hauled on shore for repairs. The sheating was stripped off, the seams recaulked, and the bottom coppered, so that in complete condition for sea, she was ready on the 24th of April to leave in company with the *O'Cain* and *Isabella* for the Sandwich Islands. With her copper bottom, the speed of the *Albatross* was so much increased that her consorts could not leave her behind. During a passage of fifty-two days the three ships were scarcely out of sight of each other, and when the weather permitted the

Captains always dined together. They all arrived at Oahu the same day.

V.[60]

A new field of commerce was opened before them, which promised better results than the fur trade of the North West. A contract for sandalwood was effected with His Majesty, of which unforseen circumstances prevented the fulfillment, chief of which was the war between England and the United States.[61]

In conformity to the new enterprise, the *Albatross* was sent to take a gang of sealers from the Farallones, finish up their unsettled business on the coast, and then cruise for some new sealing islands, where were reported to have been seen by the Russians. The other two ships were to remain at the Sandwich Islands to collect and prepare sandalwood for the Canton market, with which one ship was to load when cargo should be ready. The King furnished many natives as were requisite at the different islands, to cut and trim, and get the wood to an embarking place, and the ships employed a white to superintend the work of each gang. The journal of the *Albatross* says: "We anchored at the South Farallones the 15th of August, and took off the party with eight thousand prime fur seal skins, and all their effects." The ship then anchored at Drake's Bay to procure wood and water. At this time, there was on one of the Farallones, a sealing party left

---

[60](Boston) *Commercial Bulletin*, 17 April 1869.

[61]The navies of Britain and the United States engaged in extensive hunts, and, in some cases, captures of enemy merchant shipping. The captain of H.M.S. *Cherub* at the Hawaiian Islands in 1814 observed that there were at least a dozen American ships then engaged in the Northwest fur trade using the Islands as a place to cure skins and obtain provisions. (Captain T. Tucker to Rear Admiral Manley Dixon, 20 June 1914, Adm 1/22, Public Record Office, Kew, England.) It has yet to be demonstrated however whether the trade in pelts and sandalwood was dramatically interrupted. Certainly American traders took evasive action. H.M.S. *Racoon*, Captain W. Black, hunting for American ships in Hawaiian waters in 1814 chased rumours, and discovered that many American vessels had been sold to the Russians.

by the ship *Charon* of Boston, Captain Whitlesmore.[62] Judging from the number of parties known to have been left on these rocks or islands, within the last three years of Boston ships, and the exact number of skins which some of them have procured it will be safe to state that 150,000 fur seal skins were taken from there during that time; a fact which contrasts Spanish indolence and imbecility with the activity and enterprise of "Boston men."

At Drake's Bay the second mate and one man (Jerry Bancroft) went on shore to hunt. They came across a grizzly bear, and shot him through the head, but not killing him outright, and the bear being very close to them he seized Jerry in his hug, and before he expired bit him severely in a number of places in his left thigh and leg. The man was brought on board bleeding quite freely. His wounds were dressed, and an officer with a party was sent to bring the bear on board. They succeeded in doing so, and he proved excellent eating.

The *Albatross* returned to Oahu, October 25th, 1812, after an unsuccessful hunt for the new islands, and the journal terminates on that date. The news of the war probably reached them about that time. British ships of war soon made their appearance off the islands, where the *Charon* was captured, and the *O'Cain*, *Isabella* and *Albatross* were blockaded nearly three years.

A Royal Contract

The original contract with the King is before me, with its mark of Royalty; and as it may be considered somewhat a curiosity in its way, a verbatim copy is presented.[63]

Articles of agreement indented, made and concluded this

---

[62]More precisely Captain Isaac Whitlemore. The *Charon*, a brig, not a ship, was owned by P. T. Jackson of Boston; she sailed these waters frequently between 1807 and 1818.

[63]This sandalwood contract is the earliest extant document of its type. For discussion of its origin and further particulars, consult Gass, *Don Francisco de Paula* (1973), pp. 40-48.

twelfth day of July, in the year of our Lord one thousand eight hundred and twelve, by and between Tamaahmaah, King of the Sandwich Islands of the one part, and Nathan Winship, William Heath
Davis,[64] and Jonathan Winship, Jr. native citizens of the United
States of America, on the other part. Witnesseth:

That the said Tamaahmaah, for the considerations hereafter
mentioned and expressed, doth hereby promise, covenant and
agree, to and with the said Nathan Winship, William Heath Davis
and Jonathan Winship, Jr., and each and every of them, and each
and every of their executors, administrators and assigns, that he will
collect, or cause to be collected for them and them only, a supply of
sandalwood and cotton of the best qualities which his Islands produce; and he doth hereby give and grant unto the said Nathan
Winship, William Heath Davis, and Jonathan Winship, Jr. their
executors, administrators and assigns, the sole right and privilege of
exporting sandalwood and cotton from his Islands for the term of
ten years, and will not on any account, or in any manner whatever,
dispose of any sandalwood or cotton to any other person or persons
whomsover, or suffer any other adventurer, or adventurers, to
export any sandalwood or cotton, from any of these Islands under
his control, during the aforesaid term of ten years. In consideration
whereof, the said Nathan Winship, William Heath Davis and
Jonathan Winship, Jr., do hereby for themselves, their executors,
adminstrators and assigns, covenant, promise and agree well and
truly to pay or cause to be paid, unto the said Tamaahmaah, his suc-
cors or assigns, one-fourth of the net sales of all the sandalwood
and cotton which they may export from the Islands belonging to
Tamaahmaah, during the aforesaid term of ten years, & to make
returns in specie or such productions and manufacturers of China
as the said Tamaahmaah, his successors or assigns may think proper
to order. In testimony whereof, they have hereunto interchangeably
set their hands and seals, on this said twelfth day of July, in the year
of Our Lord, one thousand eight hundred and twelve.

> Tamaahmaah, his O mark (seal)
> William Heath Davis,   "
> Nathan Winship,   "
> Jonathan Winship, Jr.   "

---

[64]William Heath Davis, a prominent trader, went first to the Pacific as master in 1806 of
the Boston vessel *Mercury* and continued intermittently until 1818. Howay, *List of Vessels*, p.
69.

When the ships were blockaded in Honolulu, there had been a considerable quantity of the above articles sold in Canton, and there remained in the hands of J. P. Cushing, Esq., at Canton, about $80,000 to the credit of the king; waiting for an opportunity of remitting it to home with safety. Mr. Cushing chartered a Portuguese ship at last, and dispatched [it] for the Islands, but the captain delayed her departure until he lost the Monsoon, put into Manila, and waited a change, and was six months in reaching Oahu, which he ought to have done in sixty days. In consequence of the non arrival of the vessel from China with the money and goods belonging to the King, the company were placed in a awkward position which was increased by the false representations of an Englishman who had resided many years with the King (John Young, afterwards Governor of Oahu).[65] Acting for the interests of an English concern in Canton,[66] he influenced the King to believe that the company never meant to pay him, and he refused to fulfill his contract. On the arrival of the Portuguese ship [the *Mercury*] the captain was instructed by the company to deliver the China goods to the King, being one-half of the amount due him, but to keep the dollars on board, intending to retain the money in their hands as security for the King's good faith. In case however that an English ship of war should make her appearance off the harbor, the captain was then to land the specie as the property of Tamaahmaah to prevent its being captured, but by an ingenious ruse of the wily savage, was prevented. One of the King's daughters was an inmate of the residence occupied by the captains; she overheard the conversation with the Portuguese captain and the instructions he received from the company, and of course informed her royal father of the whole matter, and he soon brought the proverbial deceit and

---

[65]John Young (d. 1835), an Englishman, came to the Hawaiian Islands as boatswain of the *Eleanora,* and was detailed ashore by Kamehameha in 1792. He became principal advisor to the King in his foreign relations and played a major role in his rise to dominance.

[66]Unidentified.

cunning of the "Islander of the Pacific" into play against Yankee caution. It was usual in those days to keep a lookout from Diamond Hill[67] (a high promontory south of the harbor), for vessels heaving in sight and bound in. The signal was made by one or two natives appearing on the summit and holding up their arms. The character or size of the vessel was indicated by the number of persons exhibited, viz. for a small vessel, but one or two were seen, and proportionally for a larger; for a large man-of war, and approaching the harbor, the notice was given by an excited crowd on the mount. Having his plans secretly arranged, the signal was made, "a big ship of war coming" and the word was soon spread, she [H.M.S. *Cherub*] had English colors. The Portuguese captain hastened to land the money; the King received it and the big ship disappeared.

A contract, similar to the above one, was also made with Tamoree, king of Atovi,[68] and Oneehow, two of the Sandwich Islands which were independent of Tamaahmaah, the benefits of which were lost to the company, from the occurrence of similar unpropitious events; the kings broke faith with the company, and the contract was voided by their royal majesties' non-fulfillment thereof.

The Captains Winship returned to Boston during 1816, and retired from the sea. After passing so many years of exile from home, amid many series of storm and danger, it is not remarkable that more quiet and peaceful pursuits surrounded by social and domestic ties should have had strong attractions for them. And now, in parting with the nautical part of Captain Jonathan Winship's life, a passing tribute is due to him as a commander. The writer was personally acquainted with him, and gladly records his own opinion with the testimony

---

[67] Now Diamond Head, or Leahi.

[68] Atovi, Atooi, and Atoui are all alternate usages for Kaua'i. At the time spoken of, Kaumualii ("Tamoree") was King of Kaua'i. Recognizing Kamehameha's suzerainty in 1810, Kaumualii remained ruler in a tributary status until his death in 1824. Kuykendall, *The Hawaiian Kingdom*, I, pp. 48n, 50, 118.

of other men of the sea who knew him intimately. As an early pioneer to the Northwest Coast, and as agent for the company and chief in command of the ships of the expedition, he must frequently have been called to the firmest exertion of authority and command. His humanity is apparent from his treatment of the natives, while the health, the convenience, and as far as it could be admitted, the enjoyment of his seamen were the constant objects of his attention; kind and courteous to all, he was manly and honorable in the transactions of the multifarious business in which he was engaged whether with the savage of Nootka Sound, the savage king of the Islands, or the more civilized subject of the "Flowery Kingdom." As a seaman and navigator, he ranked among the foremost. His Brother appears to have been a counterpart of himself, and an able co-operator.

Oregon is now a part of the United States, and it would seem that if any persons could put forth claims for grants of land founded upon actual possession, building and planting, the heirs of the Winships have more than ordinary claims. The first American settlement started on the banks of the Columbia River was by them. Unfortunate circumstances in location, and the occurrence of the war, put a stop to the projected enterprise, but the fact that they were the first pioneers of civilization who planted corn, and laid the foundation of a settlement at the Columbia River, cannot be disputed. It is hoped that the Oregonians, with a knowledge of these facts, will suitably honor & perpetuate the name, by bestowing it on some fair city yet to arise in the vicinity of the first attempt.

Captain Winship was sorely disappointed at the result of his brother's attempt at the [Columbia] River; he hoped to have planted a Garden of Eden on these shores of the Pacific and made that wilderness to blossom like the rose. Repulsed on the western slope of the continent, he returned to the eastern, and here in the midst of a high civilization, where horti-

culture is considered as one of its broad footprints, he
engaged in pursuits of science, and the production of the
most beautiful things in creation. In his native town of
Brighton he laid out and cultivated the most extensive gardens of the kind then existing on the continent of America,
filled with the choicest plants and shrubbery. Millions of
pinks, roses, and every flower that can be named; it invited
the attention of all who had a taste for the purest things
under the canopy of heaven; his opinion was that a dissimination of the love for flowers was a dissimination of happi-
ness, and he scattered these flowers around with a liberal
hand. Almost every rural fete in the vicinity had been
indebted to some of these for their chief attractions. The
early manhood of Captain Winship was passed in the most
perilous pursuits, on a savage coast and in the remotest parts
of the world, which added much to the commercial knowledge and prosperity of this country—and his latter years were
peacefully spent among beds of flowers. He died among his
roses. How useful and honorable the life—how beautiful its
close.

There was also another brother, probably the eldest,
Charles Winship, who sailed from Boston in the ship
Alexander, Captain Asa Dodge, for the Northwest Coast, as
part owner and joint super cargo, in the year 1797, and subsequently, two years afterwards, as commander of the brigantine *Betsey*, to the Northwest Coast and the coasts of Upper
and Lower California, supposed to be the first vessel from
the United States to these coasts. No account of those voyages is to be found.[69] Captain Charles died at Valparaiso from
the effects of a sun-stroke during that voyage. Still another,
Captain Charles Winship, a nephew of the previous named
gentleman, was in the Pacific, in about 1819, on a sealing
voyage, and spent much time at the Falkland Islands. The

---

[69]Their careers may be followed in brief, respectively, in Howay, *List of Voyages*, pp. 34-
36, 40, 61, 169, and 41, 61.

voyage was not a successful one. The ship (which I think was the *O'Cain* of previous renown) put into Valparaiso, when by a singular coincidence, the captain's life terminated in the same manner as that of his uncle who bore the same name. Thus the descendants of the Winships may justly feel a pride in ancestors who have contributed largely to the knowledge and benefit of mankind, and extended the bonds of commerce. Others may boast of the hereditary noble blood, transmitted with stars and garters and the trappings of royalty, but in fact "ignoble blood that has crept through scoundrels ever since the flood," but these old sea kings were impelled to noble deeds by their own noble natures, born in a land of freedom; where free institutions are cherished and laudable pursuits encouraged; where men bow the knee to none "save to Heaven they pray, nor even then unless in their own way."

And here may be a fitting place to make a final mention of the two ships which have been most conspicuous in this brief history. The *O'Cain* was lost on Topocalma Shoal, off the coast of Chili, while in command of Captain Lewis Henchman, and the *Albatross* never returned to the Pacific after Captain Winship left her. The merchants of Boston sent out the fast sailing schooner *Tamaahmaah* to the Pacific at the commencement of the war, to warn the American ships on the Northwest Coast of their danger. The warning was a timely one, and those at the Russian forts, and at the Sandwich Islands, mostly remained at the neutral ports where the schooner found them. Most of their furs and some of the crews were taken down to China by the *Tamaahmaah*, under the command of Captain [Lemuel] Porter. The ship *Jacob Jones* was fitted out in Boston, and sailed during the war under the command of Captain Roberts. She was a heavily armed letter of marque, bound to Canton. During the voyage she was to fight her way whenever necessary, and probably was expected to render assistance to the North-West traders who might be at Canton. On the voyage out she had an action off the Cape of Good Hope with an English man-of-war, with the results of which I am not acquainted; but she arrived safely. To the purser of the *Jones*, D. M. Bryant, Esq., now living at South Deerfield, I am indebted for a few anecdotes and reminiscences of some of the North West men he met with in China. Captain P[orter], and some others of his stamp, used to boast of spending night after night in drunken orgies with the Russian Governor of Sitka, and of many acts of brutality toward the natives which forbear repeating. Others are mentioned more favorably. Captain John Suter, of the *Mentor*, was a pious Baptist man. Suter always had a large Bible on his cabin table, and read it in course during the voyage. Young Preble, his clerk, used to amuse himself by putting back the Captain's mark from time to time, and made him read the same chapter over and over again for a month. The old Captain thought he had a head wind all through the book of Daniel and made slow progress, but he got wonderfully well acquainted with it.

The Yankee fleet, during the winter of 1814-15, lay for some time at the first bar, below Whampoa.[70] While there they had pretty high times on board some of the ships. One night there was a company on board the *Tamaahmaah* having a gay time. Chinese girls were among them. Being filled with liquor, the captains concluded to enliven the entertainment with fire-works. After letting of a few rockets, fire was communicated to the stock on board, and then a scene ensued which was amusing to those on board the *Jones,* but anything but pleasing to those on board the schooner. During the

---

[70]The American merchantmen were then being closely watched by British men-of-war but they were also excluded from the inner waters of the Celestial Empire. In this position between war and seizure they happily passed the winter, as Phelps recounts. On Anglo-American-Chinese relations at this time, see Gerald S. Graham, *The China Station: War and Diplomacy, 1830-1860* (Oxford: Clarendon Press, 1978), pp. 13-14.

explosion and alarm, the girls jumped overboard, and were picked up by the Comprador's boat.[71]

Mr. Bryant relates the following of Captain Jonathan Winship: that while the latter was at the Islands, a brother captain wished him to fire a salute on some particular occasion which Captain Winship agreed to if the other would return gun for gun. The terms were accepted. Captain Winship had a large quantity of powder on board his ship to sell, and at it they went, firing from each ship, alternately, until the ammunition was all expended by the party who requested the salute but Winship held him to his work, and would not excuse him. He, however, offered to sell him a supply to last till sunset. The result was they hammered away all day, much to the advantage of the party who had powder to sell. But enough has been said to portray the characters and customs of the early north-west school, and here I leave them.

The Custom House Records exhibit the clearance of the following ships from Boston for the Northwest Coast, with their invoices of cargo, in addition to those already named:

Year	Ship	Captain	Invoice
1797	*Jenny*	Bowers	$17,650
1797	*Alert*	Bowles	13,090
1797	*Hazard*	Swift	15,400
1797	*Eliza*	Rowan	14,000
1797	*Alexander*	Dodge	18,500
1798	*Ulysses*	Lamb	14,000
1800	*Caroline*	Derby	18,500
1800	*Atahualpa*	Wildes	18,750
1800	*Globe* (N.W. + China)	Magee	29,253
1800	*Lucy*	Pierpont	9,718
1800	*Guatamozin*	Bumstead	18,036
1800	*Dispatch*	Dorr	19,681
1800	*Polly*	Kelly	10,631

[71]The hong merchants appointed a comprador to each ship. His function was to provide provisions and stores for the vessel.

The above will show that an invoice of about $17,000 was sufficient to procure a cargo of furs. The outward cargoes consisted mostly of tin and iron hollow ware, brass kettles, wire, beads, lead, knives, nails, small looking glasses, bar iron, hatchets, firearms, powder, flints, rum and molasses. The natives were fond of the two last articles. The molasses was given in trade—a certain number of buckets for a prime sea otter skin, &c.; the molasses in most cases consisted of the latter article and salt water in about equal proportions; perhaps the rum was doctored the same way, and was a better article at that than is now sold in the States.

During the year 1800 there was at least ten different ships belonging to Boston trading on the coast being 10-12ths of all the trade. The town of Boston at that time contained a population of less than 25,000 inhabitants. Comment is unnecessary.

The Northwest Fur Trade
by The Hon. William Sturgis

We are indebted to Elliot C. Cowdin, Esq., the president of the Mercantile Library Association of Boston, for the somewhat extended sketch of the Hon. William Sturgis's valuable lecture upon the "Northwest Fur Trade," delivered before that association, on Wednesday evening, January 21st, 1846.[1] The report was prepared by Mr. Cowdin, with much care, from the original manuscript, and can, therefore, be relied upon for its entire accuracy. Mr. Sturgis, the author of the lecture, is well known as one of the most eminent merchants of Boston; and his reputation in that city, for practical intelligence and sterling good sense, stands very high.

In commencing, the lecturer observed that, at this present moment, when the public attention is anxiously directed to the partition, or other disposition, of a large portion of the northwestern part of our continent, as a question seriously affecting both our domestic and foreign relations,[2] anything respecting that country, or its native population, assumes a more than ordinary interest.

Mr. Sturgis said that, in early life, he made several success-

---

[1]Sturgis's account was originally published in *Hunt's Merchants' Magazine*, 14 (1846): 532-38; reprinted with new introduction by F. W. Howay in *British Columbia Historical Quarterly*, 8 (1944): 11-25. Howay's version has been used here. Note that all subsequent footnotes in Appendix I are by F. W. Howay.

[2]The Oregon question, which was a burning one in 1845 and 1846.

ful voyages,[3] to what was then deemed a remote and unex-plored region, and passed a number of years among a people, at that time, just becoming known to the civilized world. His first visit to Nootka Sound was made in the last century, about twenty years after it was discovered by Captain Cook.

Though not one of the first, he was amongst those who early engaged in the *Northwest trade*, so called, and continued to carry it on, either personally or otherwise, until it ceased to be valuable.[4] He thus witnessed the growth, maximum, decrease, and, finally, its abandonment by Americans. These early visits afforded him an opportunity, too, of observing changes in the habits and manners of the Indians, effected by intercourse with a more civilized race; and he regretted to add, brought to his knowledge the injustice, violence, and bloodshed, which has marked the progress of this inter-course.[5]

Mr. Sturgis did not expect others would feel the same interest in the reminiscences that he felt, but he thought they might engage the attention of his hearers, and perhaps awaken a sympathy for the remnant of a race fast disappear-ing from the earth—victims of injustice, cruelty, and oppres-sion—and of a policy that seems to recognize *power* as the sole standard of *right*.

The hour, this evening, the lecturer proposed to devote principally to *the fur trade*, and some matters connected with it; and, in the next lecture, he should speak of the habits, peculiarities, language, and some features in the general character of the Indians. But that branch of the subject most deeply interesting to them, occurrences upon the coast

---

[3]Four voyages: 1799 in *Eliza*; 1801-2 and 1803-6 in *Caroline*; 1807 in *Atahualpa*.

[4]Bryant & Sturgis, between 1818 and 1825, owned or operated the following vessels in the trade to the Northwest Coast: *Volunteer, Cordelia, Ann, Griffon, Becket, Lascar, Mentor, Rob Roy*, and *Llama*.

[5]Sturgis was a sturdy champion of the Indians, claiming that their so-called "unpro-voked attacks" upon the trading vessels resulted from the inhuman conduct of the traders themselves.

within his own knowledge, of treatment which the Indians had received from the white men, must be postponed to some future occasion.

The Northwest trade, as far as we are concerned, has ceased to be of importance in a commercial view; but a branch of commerce, (said Mr. Sturgis,) in which a number of American vessels, and many seamen and others were constantly and profitably employed, for more than forty years[6]— which brought wealth to those engaged in it, and was probably as beneficial to the country as any commercial use of an equal amount of capital has ever been—cannot be without interest as matter of unwritten history, and may, perhaps, illustrate some principles of commerce deserving our notice and consideration.

This trade, in which our citizens largely participated, and at one period nearly monopolized, was principally limited to the sea-coast between the mouth of the Columbia river, in latitude 46°, and Cook's Inlet, in latitude 60°, to the numerous islands bordering this whole extent of coast, and the sounds, bays, and inlets, within these limits. Trade was always carried on along-side, or on board the ship, usually anchored near the shore, the Indians coming off in their canoes.[7] It was seldom safe to admit many of the natives into the ship at the same time, and a departure from this prudent course, has, in numerous instances, been followed by the most disastrous and tragical results.

The vessels usually employed were from one hundred to two hundred and fifty tons burthen, each. The time occupied for a voyage by vessels that remained upon the coast only a single season, was from twenty-two months to two years, but

---

[6]The Americans were in the trade from 1787 until at least 1836, though it ceased for all practical purposes by about 1825. Thereafter the trading vessels sought land furs, for the sea-otter had been practically exterminated.

[7]At first the trade was always from the canoes alongside; but later the Indians were allowed on board when trading.

they generally remained out two seasons, and were absent from home nearly three years. The principal object of the voyages was to procure the skins of the sea-otter, which were obtained from the natives by barter, carried to Canton, and there exchanged for the productions of the Celestial Empire, to be brought home or taken to Europe, thus completing what may be called a *trading voyage*.[8]

Beaver and common otter skins, and other small furs, were occasionally procured in considerable quantities, but in the early period they were deemed unimportant, and little attention was given to collecting them. The sea-otter skins have ever been held in high estimation by the Chinese and Russians, as an ornamental fur; but its great scarcity and consequent cost, limits the wear to the wealthy and higher classes only. A full grown prime skin, which has been stretched before drying, is about five feet long,[9] and twenty-four to thirty inches wide, covered with very fine fur, about three-fourths of an inch in length, having a rich jet black, glossy surface, and exhibiting a silver color when blown open. Those are esteemed the finest skins which have some white hairs interspersed and scattered over the whole surface, and a perfectly white head. Mr. Sturgis said that it would now give him more pleasure to look at a splendid sea-otter skin, than to examine half the pictures that are stuck up for exhibition, and puffed up by pretended connoisseurs. In fact, excepting a beautiful woman and a lovely infant, he regarded them as among the most attractive natural objects that can be placed before him.

The sea-otter has been found only in the North Pacific. The earliest efforts on record to collect furs in that region, were made by Russians from Kamschatka,[10] who, in the early

---

[8]The trade with the Indians was a means to an end—to secure a medium of exchange for Chinese goods.

[9]Jewitt (Brown, ed., p. 121) says a prime skin was one that would reach from a man's chin to his feet. On the sea-otter see Ogden, *The California Sea Otter Trade* (1941), p. 4; Busch, *War Against The Seals*, pp. 3-4.   [10]Bering and Chirikov.

part of the last century, visited, for this purpose, the Kurile and other islands that lie near the northern coasts of Asia. After the expedition of Behring & Co., in 1741, these excursions were slowly extended to other groups between the two continents, and when Cook, in 1778, explored these northern regions, he met with Russian adventurers upon several of the islands in proximity with the American shore. It was, however, the publication of Cook's northern voyages in 1785,[11] that gave the great impulse to the Northwest fur trade, and drew adventurers from several nations to that quarter.

The published journal of Captain King, who succeeded to the command of one of the ships after the death of Captains Cook and Clark,[12] and his remarks, setting forth the favorable prospects for this trade, doubtless roused the spirit of adventure. Between the time of the publication referred to, in 1785,[13] and the close of 1787, expeditions were fitted out from Canton, Macao, Calcutta and Bombay, in the East, London and Ostend in Europe, and from Boston in the United States. In 1787, the first American expedition was fitted out, and sailed from Boston. It consisted of the ship *Columbia*, of two hundred and twenty, and the sloop *Washington*, of ninety tons burthen—the former commanded by John Kenrick, the latter by Robert Gray.[14]

Mr. Sturgis deemed it scarcely possible, in the present age, when the departure or return of ships engaged in distant voyages is an every-day occurrence, to appreciate the magnitude of this undertaking, or the obstacles and difficulties that had to be surmounted in carrying it out.[15]

---

[11]Cook's *Third Voyage* was published in 1784. It is in three volumes; the first two are by Captain Cook—the third, by Captain King, is not a journal, but a narrative.

[12]Captain Charles Clerke.

[13]1784. James Hanna, the first maritime fur-trader, sailed from Macao, April 15, 1785.

[14]The *Columbia* was of 212 8/95 tons. *Kendrick*, not *Kenrick*.

[15]The expedition failed financially not so much on account of the unknown and inherent difficulties as by reason of the incapacity or worse of its commander, Captain John Kendrick.

He said, were he required to select any particular event in the commercial history of our country, to establish our reputation for bold enterprise and persevering energy, in commercial pursuits, he should point to this expedition of the *Columbia* and *Washington*. Many of the obstacles and dangers were clearly pointed out, showing that it was then viewed as an extraordinary undertaking. A medal was struck upon the occasion, and some impressions taken out in the vessels for distribution. The lecturer briefly described it, and exhibited to the audience a *facsimile* of one preserved in the Department of State at Washington. On one side of this medal was engraved "Columbia and Washington: commanded by J. Kenrick," with a representation of the two vessels; on the reverse was the following inscription: "Fitted at Boston, N. America, for the Pacific Ocean, by J. Burrell, C. Brown, C. Bulfinch, J. Darby, C. Hatch, J. M. Pintard, 1787."[16]

Captain Kenrick, who was entrusted with the command of the expedition, was a bold, energetic, experienced seaman. His management justified the confidence reposed in him, but he was fated never to return.[17]

The project of engaging in the fur trade of the North Pacific, from this country, was first brought forward by the celebrated American traveller, Ledyard.[18] In his erratic wanderings, he entered on board the ship *Resolution*, as corporal of marines, with Captain Cook, upon his last voyage. After his return, he made repeated attempts to get an outfit for a voyage to the Northwest Coast. In 1784, three years previous to Kenrick's expedition, he induced Robert Morris to engage

[16]One of these medals in silver is in the possession of the Massachusetts Historical Society. A photograph of it is to be found in F. W. Howay, *Voyages of the "Columbia"* (Boston: Massachusetts Historical Society, 1941), facing p. 162. Again, *Kenrick* should be *Kendrick*; *Burrell* should be *Barrell*; and *C. Brown* should be *S. Brown*.

[17]Kendrick does not by any means measure up to this laudation; and his owners found that their confidence was misplaced. In plain English he stole the *Washington*, one of the vessels entrusted to his care.

[18]Ledyard was only a dreamer of impracticable dreams. The impetus that set the maritime fur-trade in motion came from the reading of Captain Cook's *Third Voyage*.

in the undertaking. But for some cause, now unknown, the enterprise was abandoned, as were similar ones in France and England. The unfortunate Ledyard seemed doomed to disappointment in whatever he undertook. The life of this remarkable man shows that respectable talents, united with great energy and perseverance of character, may be comparatively valueless to the possessor, and useless to the world, from the want of well-balanced mind, which, unfortunately, was the fatal deficiency in Ledyard.

Nearly all the early and distinguished navigators, who discovered and explored the northern regions of the Pacific, met the fate that too often awaits the pioneers in bold and hazardous undertakings, and found a premature death, by violence or disaster, or disease brought on by incessant toil and exposure.[19]

Behring, a Danish navigator in the service of Russia, who commanded the expedition just mentioned, was wrecked in 1741, upon an island that bears his name, and perished miserably in the course of the winter. He was the first navigator known to have passed through the strait that separates Asia from America; and Cook, who was the next to sail through it, in a commendable spirit of justice, gave to this strait the name of the unfortunate Behring. The fate of Cook is well known. He was killed by the natives of the Sandwich Islands, of which group he was the discoverer.

Mr. Sturgis said he had stood upon the spot where Cook fell, in Karakakooa Bay, and conversed with the natives who were present at the time of the massacre. They uniformly expressed regret and sorrow for his death, but insisted that it was caused by his own imprudence.

---

[19]Bering died of scurvy on Bering Isle, in 1741; Captain Cook was killed at Kealekekua Bay, Hawaii, by the natives in February, 1779; Captain Charles Clerke died of tuberculosis in Bering Sea in 1779; Captain John Kendrick was accidentally killed at Honolulu on December 12, 1795; Solomon, his second son, was killed by the Haidas when they captured the *Resolution*, tender of the *Jefferson*, in 1793; Captain Simon Metcalfe and his son, Robert, were murdered by the Haidas when they captured the *Eleonora*, in 1794, and his eldest son, Thomas H. Metcalfe, was killed by the Hawaiians at Kawaihai, Hawaii, when they captured the *Fair American*.

The lecturer next gave an interesting account of the loss of two French vessels fitted out in 1785,[20] on a voyage of discovery and exploration, which, after visiting the northwest coast of America, departed from Sydney, in New South Wales, early in 1788, and nothing more was heard from them until 1826, when a wreck and some articles were found at the island of Malicolo, in the South Pacific, that left no doubt but the unfortunate Frenchmen perished there.[21]

Vancouver, an able British navigator, was sent out by his government in 1790, to receive Nootka Sound from the Spaniards, and explore the whole western coast of North America. The chart prepared by him is the most accurate of any at the present day. With a constitution shattered by devotion to his arduous duties, he returned to England in 1794, and sunk into an early grave.[22]

Mr. Sturgis said he had already remarked that Kendrick was fated never to return. After remaining with both vessels two seasons on the northwest coast, he sent the *Columbia* home, in charge of Captain Gray, and remained himself in the sloop *Washington*.[23] He continued in her several years, trading on the coast and at the Sandwich Islands.[24]

In 1792, while lying in the harbor of Honolulu, at one of these islands, and receiving, upon his birthday, a complimentary salute from the captain of an English trading vessel

---

[20]*La Boussole* and *L'Astrolabe*, under the command of La Pérouse.

[21]In September, 1827, Captain P. Dillon found on the island of Vanikoro, now Mallicolo, iron, copper, and silver relics of La Pérouse's vessels, and heard from the natives the story of their wrecks.

[22]Vancouver was sent out to, amongst other duties, receive the restoration of the lands on the Northwest Coast of which Spain had dispossessed Meares and his associates. Vancouver returned to England in September, 1795, and died May 18, 1798, aged 40.

[23]The slippery conduct of Kendrick after 1790 accounts for his non-return to Boston. The fates had no hand in it. For light on this matter see Howay, *Voyages of the "Columbia,"* pp. 470, 485, 490, 494f. On the first voyage, 1787-90, Kendrick spent only one season on the coast; the *Columbia* and *Washington* arrived at the end of season of 1788 and Kendrick left the coast at the end of the season of 1789.

[24]Sturgis might have added: "Treating the *Washington* as his own property and steadily going further into debt."

anchored near, he was instantly killed by a shot carelessly left in one of the guns fired on the occasion.[25]

Captain Gray reached home in the *Columbia*, in the summer of 1790,[26] and thus completed the first circumnavigation of the globe under the American flag. He was immediately fitted out for a second voyage in the same ship, and it was during this voyage that he discovered, entered, and gave the name to the Columbia river, a circumstance now relied upon as one of the strongest grounds to maintain our claim to the Oregon Territory. He died abroad some years ago.

Mr. Sturgis here observed that it would bring some of the events of which he had spoken quite near our own time, to mention that in the street in which we are, (Federal-street,) the name of "Gray" may be seen upon the door of a house nearly opposite Milton Place,[27] which house is now occupied by the widow and daughters of Captain Gray, the discoverer of the Columbia river, and the first circumnavigator who bore the flag of our country in triumph round the world.

The voyage of the *Columbia* was not profitable to her owners, in a pecuniary view, but it opened the way for other adventures, which were commenced on her return. In 1791, there were seven vessels from the United States in the North Pacific, in pursuit of furs.[28] For various reasons, the American traders so far gained the ascendancy, that at the close of the last century, with the exception of the Russian establish-

---

[25]This paragraph is quite wrong. Kendrick was accidentally killed on December 12, 1795, as stated; but it was not his birthday; the occasion of the salute was the victory which had been won by the army of Oahu over the invaders from Kauai.

[26]August 8, 1790.

[27]83 Federal Street, Boston, where lived Mrs. Martha Gray, the widow of Captain Robert Gray. See *Washington Historical Quarterly*, 21 (1930), p. 11. The date and place of Captain Gray's death are uncertain. E. G. Porter says he died in 1806 at Charleston, S.C. (*New England Magazine*, June, 1892, p. 488); Mrs. Martha Gray, in her petition of January 17, 1846, states that she "was left a widow nearly forty years ago"; and the Committee of the House reporting thereon find that Captain Gray "died in the summer of 1806." Intensive search has not revealed any more definite information.

[28]*Columbia, Eleanora, Grace, Hancock, Hope*, and *Washington*. Perhaps Sturgis included the *Adventure*, which was built in the winter of 1791-92.

ments on the northern part of the coast, the whole trade was in our hands, and so remained until the close of the war with Great Britain, in 1815. This trade was confined almost exclusively to Boston. It was attempted, unsuccessfully, from Philadelphia and New York, and from Providence and Bristol, in Rhode Island. Even the intelligent and enterprising merchants of Salem, failed of success;[29] some of them, however, were interested in several of the most successful northwestern voyages carried on from Boston. So many of the vessels engaged in this trade belonged here, the Indians had the impression that Boston was our whole country. Had any one spoken to them of *American* ships, or *American* people, he would not have been understood. We were only known as Boston ships, and *Boston* people.[30]

In 1801, the trade was most extensively, though not most profitably prosecuted; that year, there were 15 vessels on the coast,[31]and in 1802 more than 15,000 sea-otter skins were collected, and carried to Canton. But the competition was so great, that few of the voyages were then profitable, and some were ruinous. Subsequently, the war with Great Britain interrupted the trade for a time; but after the peace in 1815, it was resumed, and flourished for some years. The difficulties and uncertainty in procuring furs became so serious, that in 1829 the business north of California was abandoned.[32]

Besides the 15,000 skins collected by the American traders in 1802, probably the Russians obtained 10,000 the same year within their hunting limits, making an aggregate of 25,000 in one season. Mr. Sturgis said he had personally col-

---

[29]It is scarcely correct to say that the Salem merchants "failed of success" in the maritime fur trade; they did not enter it. The *New Hazard* in 1811-12 was the solitary exception.

[30]In the Chinook jargon anything American is called "Boston."

[31]*Atahualpa, Betsy, Catherine, Caroline, Charlotte, Despatch, Enterprise, Globe, Guatimozin, Hazard, Lavinia, Litteler, Lucy, Mary, Manchester, Polly,* and *Three Sisters.*

[32]After about 1825 the American vessels sought land furs—the sea-otter had been practically exterminated. But when these vessels entered the land trade they met the energetic opposition of the Hudson's Bay Company, and quickly disappeared.

lected 6000 in a single voyage,[33] and he once purchased 560 of prime quality in half a day. At the present time, the whole amount collected annually within the same limits does not exceed 200, and those of very ordinary quality.

The commercial value of the sea-otter skin, like other commodities, has varied with the changes in the relation of supply and demand.

The narrative of Cook's voyage shows the value of a prime skin to have been, at the time of that voyage, $120. In 1802, when the largest collection was made, the average price of large and small skins, at Canton, was only about $20 each. At the present time, those of first quality would sell readily at $150. Some seventy or eighty ordinary California skins, brought home a few months ago, were sold here at nearly $60 each, to send to the north of Europe.[34]

Mr. Sturgis said the trade on the coast was altogether a barter trade. It consisted in part of blankets, coarse cloths, great-coats, firearms and ammunition, rice, molasses, and biscuit, coarse cottons, cutlery, and hard-ware, a great variety of trinkets, &c; in fact, everything that one can can imagine.[35] Copper has long been known, and highly prized by the Indians. The lecturer observed that he had seen pieces of virgin copper among the different tribes, that weighed 50 or 60

---

[33]This is probably an error of the reporter. Sturgis's best voyage—that of the *Caroline*, in 1803-4, when he made the successful venture with the ermine skins—produced 2,500 sea-otter skins. The reference is to the voyage of the *Pearl*, Captain John Suter, in 1808-9; in two seasons on the coast that ship obtained 6,000 sea-otter skins, the high-water mark.

[34]In 1792 John Hoskins wrote: "The very best Skins at retail will not fetch more than thirty dollars and at wholesale from six to twenty-five dollars." In 1795 Kendrick's 1,063 skins and 640 tails only brought $16,755—about $15 each: Howay, *The Voyages of the "Columbia"*, pp. 480, 488. The Californian sea-otter skins were usually obtained by poaching or by surreptitious trade.

[35]Sturgis has omitted rum from his list of trading goods. When the *Boston* was captured in 1803, she had twenty puncheons of rum, about 2,000 gallons, on board for trade, besides a miscellaneous assortment of other intoxicating liquors. See on this and the trade generally, F. W. Howay, "The Introduction of Intoxicating Liquor amongst the Indians of the Northwest Coast," *British Columbia Historical Quarterly* (1942): 157-69.

pounds each. It was put to no use, but still was considered very valuable, and a person having a few pieces was deemed a wealthy man.[36]

The natives had no currency.[37] But the skin of the ermine, found in limited numbers upon the northern part of the continent, was held in such universal estimation, and of such uniform value, among many tribes, that it in a measure supplied the place of currency. The skin of this little slender animal is from eight to twelve inches in length, perfectly white, except the tip of the tail, which is jet black.

Urged by some Indian friends, in 1802, Mr. Sturgis obtained and sent home a fine specimen, with a request that a quantity should be ordered at the annual Leipsic fair, where he supposed they might be obtained. About 5,000 were procured, which he took out with him on the next voyage, and arrived at Kigarnee, one of the principal trading places on the coast, early in 1804. Having previously encouraged the Indians to expect them, the first question was, if he had "clicks," (the Indian name for the ermine skin) for sale, and being answered in the affirmative, great earnestness was manifested to obtain them, and it was on that occasion that he purchased 560 prime sea-otter skins, at that time worth $50 apiece at Canton, in a single forenoon, giving for each five ermine skins, that cost less than thirty cents each in Boston. He succeeded in disposing of all his ermines at the same rate, before others carried them out—but in less than two years from that time, one hundred of them would not bring a sea-otter skin.

Among a portion of the Indians, the management of trade

---

[36]The native copper came from Copper River, Alaska; it was made into knives, swords, whistles, and rattles, and sometimes beaten out into a sheet to form an ornamental breastplate highly esteemed as a symbol of wealth and distinction. A representation of one of these "coppers" is given in George M. Dawson, *Report on the Queen Charlotte Islands* (Montreal, 1880), p. 135.

[37]Amongst the Haidas, Nootkans, and Chinooks at any rate, the dentalium shell served as a sort of currency.

is entrusted to the women. The reason given by the men was, that women could talk with the white men *better* than they could, and were willing to talk *more*.[38]

When the natives had a number of skins for sale, it was usual to fix a price for those of the first quality as a standard, which required a great deal of haggling. In addition to the staple articles of blankets, or cloth, or muskets, &c., that constituted this price, several smaller articles were given as presents, nominally, but in reality formed part of the price. Of these small articles, different individuals would require a different assortment: a system of equivalents was accordingly established. For instance, an iron pot and an axe were held to be of equal value—so of a knife and a file, a pocket looking-glass and a pair of scissors.

Mr. Sturgis next alluded to the various efforts made by the Indians to obtain a more valuable article than the established equivalent. To avoid trouble, which would certainly follow if he yielded in a single instance, he said he had found it necessary to waste hours in a contest with a woman about articles of no greater value than a skein of thread or a sewing needle. From various causes, the northwest trade was liable to great fluctuations. The laws of supply and demand were frequently disregarded, and prices consequently often unsettled. He had seen prime sea-otter skins obtained for articles that did not cost fifty cents at home, and had seen given for them articles that cost here nearly twice as much as the skins would sell for in China.

To secure success with any branch of business, it must be undertaken with intelligence, and steadily prosecuted. Men of sanguine temperaments are often led by reports of great profits made by others, to engage in a business of which they are ignorant, or have not adequate means to carry it on, and thus involve themselves in loss or ruin. These truths Mr. Sturgis deemed strikingly illustrated by the northwest trade.

---

[38]Amongst the Haidas the women had the management of the trade with the vessels.

While most of those who had rushed into this trade without knowledge, experience, or sufficient capital to carry it on, have been subjected to such serious losses, they were compelled to abandon it; to all who pursued it systematically and perseveringly, for a series of years, it proved highly lucrative. Among those who were the most successful in this trade, were the late firm of J. & T. H. Perkins, J. & Thos. Lamb, Edward Dorr & Sons, Boardman & Pope, Geo. W. Lyman, Wm. H. Boardman, the late Theodore Lyman, and several others, each of whom acquired a very ample fortune.

These fortunes were not acquired, as individual wealth not unfrequently is, at the expense of our own community, by a tax upon the whole body of consumers, in the form of enhanced prices, often from adventitious causes. They were obtained abroad by giving to the Indians articles which they valued more than their furs, and then selling those furs to the Chinese for such prices as they are willing to pay; thus adding to the wealth of the country, at the expense of foreigners, all that was acquired by individuals beyond the usual return for the use of capital, and suitable compensation for the services of those employed. This excess was sometimes very large. Mr. Sturgis said that more than once he had known a capital of $40,000, employed in a northwest voyage, yield a return exceeding $150,000. In one instance, an outfit not exceeding $50,000, gave a gross return of $284,000. The individual who conducted the voyage is now a prominent merchant of Boston.[39]

In conclusion, the lecturer gave a brief account of the two great fur companies. In 1785 an association of merchants was formed in Siberia for the purpose of collecting furs in the North Pacific. In 1799 they were chartered under the name of the "Russian American Company," with the exclusive

---

[39]Probably the reference is to the voyage of the *Pearl*, in 1808-9. The value of ship, outfit, and cargo was about $40,000, and the return cargo sold at auction in 1810 for $261,343.18, gross.

privilege of procuring furs within the Russian limits, (54° 40')
for a period of twenty years, which has since been extended.[40]

The furs collected are sent across Siberia to Katska, the
great mart for peltries in the northern part of China, or to St.
Petersburg. For a number of years the company obtained a
large portion of their supplies from American vessels, giving
in return seal-skins and other furs, and latterly, bills on St.
Petersburg.

The treatment of the agents and servants of the company,
to the Indians, has been of the most atrocious and revolting
character.

The British Hudson Bay Company was chartered by
Charles II, in 1669,[41] with the grant of the exclusive use and
control of a very extensive though not well-defined country,
north and west of Canada. This uncertainty as to limits, led
to the formation of an association of merchants in Canada in
1787, called the "Northwest Company," for carrying on the
fur trade without the supposed boundaries of the Hudson
Bay Company.

Those in the service of these concerns soon came in collision. Disputes and personal violence followed. At length, in
June, 1816, a pitched battle was fought near a settlement that
had been made by Lork Selkirk, upon the Red River, under a
grant from the Hudson Bay Company, between the settlers
and a party in the service of the Northwest Company,
between the settlers and a party in the service of the Northwest Company, in which Governor Semple and seventeen of
his men were killed. This roused the attention of the British

---

[40]The United American Company, which was a fusion of the Shelekof-Golikof Company and the Muilnikof Company, was founded in 1798, and in 1799 obtained a charter as
the Russian American Company. Clarence L. Andrews, *The Story of Alaska* (Caldwell,
Idaho, 1938), p. 69.

[41]The Hudson's Bay charter is dated May 2, 1670. The North West Company, a combi-
nation of persons already in the fur trade, is usually said to have been formed in 1783. It
traded within and without the chartered limits of the Hudson's Bay Company, utterly obliv-
ious of the "uncertainty" thereof.

government, and in 1821, the two companies were united, or rather, the Northwest Company was merged into the Hudson Bay Company. Previous to this, however, the Northwest Company had, in 1806, established trading posts beyond the Rocky Mountains.[42] During the last war with Great Britain, they got possession of Mr. Astor's settlement at the mouth of the Columbia, and extended their posts on several branches of that river. These establishments being united, it infused new life, and their operations have since been conducted with increased vigor. They have now, practically, a monopoly of the fur trade, from 42° to 54° 40', on the western sea-board, and from 49° to the Northern Ocean, upon the rest of the American continent.

With the exception of the British East India Company, the Hudson Bay Company is the most extensive and powerful association of individuals for private emolument, now in existence, and their influence has hitherto prevented an adjustment of the Oregon question. Mr. Sturgis said he did not speak from mere conjecture, when he affirmed that it would have been settled months ago, upon the line suggested by him in a previous lecture before this association, and to the satisfaction of the people of both countries, but for the selfish interference of this company. Should disastrous consequences follow the delay in settling this question, it will add another to the numerous evils that have already resulted from great commercial monopolies.

The whole business of collecting furs upon our western continent, without the acknowledged limits of the United States, is now monopolized by two great corporations, the Russian and British Fur Companies.

After the peace in 1815, the British Northwest Company-partly in consequence of the monopoly of the East India Company—were compelled to seek the aid of American

---

[42]Fort McLeod was founded in 1805; three other posts were constructed in 1806-7.

merchants and American vessels, in carrying on an important branch of their business. For a number of years, all the
supplies for British establishments, west of the Rocky
Mountains, were brought from London to Boston, and carried hence to the mouth of the Columbia in American ships,
and all their collections of furs sent to Canton, consigned to
an American house, and the proceeds shipped to England or
the United States, in the same vessels; a fact which speaks
loudly in favor of the freedom of our institutions and the
enterprise of our merchants. Our respected fellow citizens,
Messrs. Perkins & Co., furnished the ships, and transacted
the business.[43]

We may state, on the authority of Mr. Cowdin, that the lecture was listened to with unbroken attention and merited
approbation, by a numerous and highly intelligent audience.
Very many of the most prominent merchants and distinguished citizens of Boston were in attendance, among whom
was the venerable Thomas H. Perkins. As a matter of "unwritten history," the lecture is indeed very valuable—inasmuch as
it imparts a knowledge of the commercial enterprises of by-
gone days, interesting in a high degree, and not accessible in
any other form. In fact, it was just what a lecture should be—
the result of large experience and practical wisdom, set forth
in a clear, methodical, and comprehensive manner.

It is to be regretted that more of our prominent merchants
are not brought forward in this capacity, for it is from them
that the younger branches of the mercantile community
derive their best lessons of the duties and responsibilities of
commercial life.

---

[43]Under this arrangement (see *Correspondence of Foreign Office and Hudson's Bay Company...Confidential...*[Ottawa, 1899], pp. 10-11), the North West Company sent furs to
Canton in the following ships of J. & T. H. Perkins: *Alexander,* 1817; *Levant,* 1818; *Nautilus,*
1819; *Levant,* 1820; *Alexander,* 1821; *Houqua,* 1822. See F. W. Howay, "A List of Trading
Vessels in the Maritime Fur Trade," in *Transactions of the Royal Society of Canada,* Section
1933, pp. 133, 141; ibid., 1934, pp. 18, 22, 36.

William Sturgis on the American Vessels and the Maritime Trade

To those who are concern'd in the North West Trade the following information & remarks may be somewhat interesting—I shall briefly state the number of vessells employ'd— the quantity of Furs collected & the average price at Canton, each year and also the price of skins & articles most in demand on the Coast & the causes of the great fluctuations in the value of those articles. I shall likewise mention the casualties which have annually occur'd. ...

1799

Description Vessells	Name	Masters	Where belonging to	Number of Skins
Ship	*Eliza*	Rowan	Boston	2,800
"	*Ulysses*	Lamb	"	1,200
"	*Hancock*	Crocker	"	1,700
"	*Despatch*	Breck	"	1,400
"	*Dove*	Duffin	Canton	1,000
"	*Cheerfull*	Beck	"	700
Sloop	*Dragon*	Cleveland	"	2,200
			Total	11,000

which sold at an average price for Twenty-five Dollars for Skin...

This document is from S. W. Jackman, ed., *The Journal of William Sturgis* (Victoria, BC: Sono Nis Press, 1987), pp. 113-26. Internal evidence would date this document after 1804, according to Jackman, who explained that, "it may well have been written in Boston and the manuscript, from which the present text is taken, is original rather than a later copy. The manuscript is very fragile and in poorish condition. The omission of words in the present text are (sic) a consequence of their being indecipherable owing to dampness and the like" (p. 113).

When we arriv'd on the Coast in the *Eliza* /Feb. 13th/—the articles most in demand were Blue board cloth, & red—Muskets—Great Coats—Powder, Wire, Axes & coarse Cutlery— we commenc'd trade by giving two fathoms of blue cloth for a prime skin, or a musket for three skins—wire beads, axes, cutlery &c now [?] given for Small skins & Tails—before the end of the season this price [?] was advanc'd to five fathoms cloth. In consequence the very injudicious & improper conduct of some of the Gentlemen who had the direction of the business, this misconduct was particularly notorious in one instance which fell under my immediate observation—the *Ulysses* & *Despatch* met together at a Port call'd Tsisscene where the Natives had about 250 skins for sale—both began trade at two fathoms & small assortment of trifling articles of little value, every skin might have been purchased in two days at this price & each ship had an equal number—but unfortunately the commanders were at variance & each was anxious to injure the other, the consequences was, the price of skins was rais'd, in the course of an hour from 2 fathoms to 5 & the natives, finding such a competition were averse to selling their skins lest the price should rise still more & and we were ten days detained instead of two & paid 150 per cent more than we need to have done—the news of this transaction spread rapidly among the neighbouring tribes & at every port we visited afterwards we were compell'd to give the same price . . . 2 fathoms red cloth was considered equal to 3 of blue & and was in demand. The Cargoes of the Vessells from Canton consisted chiefly of great coats made of thin serge, some cloth, China made trunks & chests & various trinkets, some of which sold well- fortunately, there were not a sufficient number of muskets on the coast to meet the demand. Of course they rose in value towards the close of the season, when a good one would sell for sometimes 5 skins on many parts of the Coast.

This year the following circumstances gave rise to that fondness for bread rice & molasses they (the natives) have since manifested—which now make so considerable part of a

NW Cargo—when the *Eliza* was at Kigarne in the month of March a large number of natives had assembled in the cove where she lay, about 7 or 8 miles above the villiage to which they usually retir'd at night—a gale of wind setting in from the southeast which lasted 3 days detain'd them in the cove & their provissions were soon expended—Captain Rowan ordered some rice to be boil'd & after mixing a considerable quantity of molasses with it distributed it among them, they found it very palatable & were pleas'd with it—shortly after they applied to purchase some, but having only a sufficiency for ship stores we could not sell them much as a proof of the value of molasses with them at this time. I have frequently seen them, when we were giving 3 fathoms broad cloth for a skin, take 2 fathoms or a bottle of molasses in preference—after the business of the day was over if they had traded briskly & sold a large number of skins Captain Rowan would frequently distribute part of Bbl. bread amng thm, with which they were much gratified.

The only sinister event which happened this year was at Cumshewars—a boat from the ship *Cheerfull* was imprudently sent on shore for wood—the natives attack'd the crew & with daggers & muskets massacred the Second Officer & 2 men, the others got off to the ship—all the Vessells left the coast previous to the 10th September....

1800

Description Vessells	Name	Masters	Where belonging to	Number of Skins
Ship	*Alert*	Bowles	Boston	2,400
"	*Terry*	Bowers	D——	2,200
"	*Alexander*	Dodge	D——	1,200
Schnooer	*Rover*	Davidson	D——	2,000
Ship	*Dove*	Duffin	Canton	2,000
"	*Flarard*	Swift	Boston—wintered on the coast	——
			Total	9,800

Sold at Canton for 22 dollars per skin.

The articles in demand this season were similar to those of last year—3 fathoms cloth was the greatest price given on many parts of the coast. Skins were bought for 2—. Some bread was sold at 5 skins pr. Hhd and rice and molasses at 8 Gallons of either, pr. Skin. Russia sheeting sold quick at 5 fathoms pr skin—Blankets—3 for a skin and India cottons for small skins and tails.

The *Alexander* visited a Port in Lat. 51° called Newetteo which had never before been known to the Americans—Captain Dodge procured there 600 skins which did not cost a fathom cloths each—I mention this circumstance as it first opened a place to the Americans where they have since collected 1500 to 2000 skins annually. Dodge was piloted into the place by a Captain Stewart, residing at the Sandwich Islands.

Captain Dodge on his outward passage landed a number of men on the Island of St. Ambrose, near Massafuero, for the purpose of killing seals, intending to return there after leaving the N.W. Coast—this he attempted to do; but having a long passage and being short of provisions, he leapt overboard in a fit of despair and was drowned—the ship immediately proceeded for the Sandwich Islands, and on her passage from thence to China the People on board carelessly set fire to a cask of Powder in the cabin, blew off the qr. deck and badly wounded several of the ship's company. She eventually arrived home, but made a bad voyage which I think may be entirely imputed to their embracing too many objects at once. A North West Voyage should never be blended with any other. It is of itself a very arduous undertaking and ought to command a man's undivided attention.

The Schooner *Rover*—Captain Davidson, belonging to Miss Dorry of Boston, left the Sandwich Islands with 2,000 skins on board and was never heard of afterward, it was conjectured she foundered in a Typhoon in which the *Jenny* lost her mizen mast.

Captain Bowers in the *Jenny*, anchored in a small harbour in Chatham Strait where there was no appearance of any Indians—a boats crew, with the first officer were sent on shore for wood—while they were employed in cutting it, a number of natives, who were lurking in the woods, rushed between them and their arms and with spears killed the Boatswain and three men. The officer took to the water and swam for the ship. The Indians fired at him with the muskets belonging to the boat and shot him through the arm. He was however saved by a Boat from the ship and recovered.

A few pieces of thick Duffiles were sold to the natives this year and they soon found the difference between this and common thin cloth and gave it a decided preference. They also prefered a thick blanket to a fathom of thin cloth—muskets still kept their value.

The erroneous idea which was cherished respecting the immense profits made in the N.W. Trade induced many adventurers to engage in it without either information or Capital. The consequence was what anyone acquainted with the business might foresee, that almost all of them made losing voyages.

I was at this time in the *Caroline* with Captain Derby. We arrived on the Coast the first vessel, 22nd January, and began to purchase skins on very moderate terms, giving 3 fathoms think blue cloth or 2 of red or 3 blankets for a prime skin, a musket for 3 skins—Great coats a skin each—before the end of April the Vessells were all on, the Brig *Polly* was the last that arriv'd—Several of them were only fitted for one season & a spectator would have thought their sole object was to get rid of their cargoes as soon as possible without minding what they got in return, so wantonly & unnecessarily did they squander it away that even the Natives, who were reaping the profits of their misconduct, openly censur'd their proceedings & laugh'd at their folly—in the months of May and June there was given at Kigarnee & in its neighborhood by the

Brig *Polly*, Ships *Lucy* & *Charlotte*, Brig *Lavinia* & several others, 10 fathoms blue cloth for a skin—3 muskets 1 skin, & other articles in proportion, except Bread, rice & molasses of which they had but little—those vessells that intended wintering were compell'd to spend their time in visiting the unfrequented ports where they procur'd but few skins, but got them on more reasonable terms—Rice & molasses sold at 10 Galls of either for a skin & more was wanted than the quantity on the coast, but bread was sold towards the close of the season for 3 skins per Hhd.-$1000 in rice & molasses, was of more value & would bring a greater number of skins than $10,000 would bring in cloth etc.

1801

Description Vessells	Name	Masters	Where belonging to	Number of Skins
Ship	*Flarard*	Swift	Boston	3,200—
				2 seasons
"	*Charlotte*	Ingersoll	Do	1,500} also
				carried down 1,000
"	*Gautamonin*	Bunkhead	Do	900
"	*Lucy*	Pierfront	Do	700
"	*Despatch*	Dorry	Do	1,300
"	*Enterprise*	Hubbell	N. York	600
"	*Bell Savage*	Ockington	Boston	600—
				year following
Brig	*Lavinia*	Holbrook	Bristol/RI/	2,000
	Littiller	Doro	Boston	1,500
	Polly	Kelby	Do	700
				13,000
Ship	*Globe*	Magee	Do	
	Caroline	Derby	Do	Sold
	Atahualpa	Wild	Do}Wintered	at
	Manchester	Brice	Phila	an average
	Unicorn	Barber	London	of 21
				Dolls

The ship *Bell Savage* was this year attacked in a very daring manner, by the natives of a Port in Lat. 52° 32' called Wacosks- she was under weigh standing down the Sound with a light air of wind- numbers of Indians were standing in her chains on both sides and one chief was sitting on the Taffrel inboard—the boarding nets were up, but the natives had privately cut away the seirings that confined them to the rail, and the chief, from the traffrel, giving the war hoop as a signal, they rushed on board and in an instant had possession of the deck. Part of the crew with the officers got into the forecastle—the Indians took possession of the cabin where they massacred, in a most shocking manner, the cabin boy and a young woman—fortunately they had no fire arms and a few discharges from the forecastle at length compelled them to quit the ship—the number killed were 3 men one woman and a boy, and several others were badly wounded—what number of Indians fell could not be ascertained but probably not many after the greater part of them had quit her, one less courageous than the rest stood on the taffrel hesitating about jumping overboard. Captain Ockington came up and ran a bayonet into his back with such force that he was unable to withdraw it and the Indian went to the bottom, musket, bayonet and all—several months after this, Captain Ingersoll in the *Charlotte* went to this place with the avowed design of revenging this attack and five of the principal chiefs were seduced on board under the specious appearance of friendship and massacred in the cabin. I am sorry to say that several of the people sacrificed on this occasion belonged to another Tribe and were by no means implicated in the attack on the *Bell Savage*—the friends of these unfortunate men some belonged to the Chelasher Tribe, were of course, much exasperated and waited impatiently for an opportunity of revenge and it was not long before one offered in October, Captain Magee, in the *Globe*, went into a small harbour, near the residence of these people, intending to pass the winter there, as

Swift had the preceding one—the ship was moored to the trees and the long boat hauled on shore to repair—the place chosen for this purpose was not a cable's length from the ship but an intervening point of land prevented their seeing her. Captain Magee, the carpenter and a boy were on shore—a canoe with 4 natives came into the cove, went along side the ship and stayed there some time; they then went on shore, and so far was Captain Magee from apprehending any danger that he called them to him to make some enquiries on the subject of trade—the carpenters account of what followed was this—that as he was on his knees caulking the boat, he was alarmed by the report of a pistol and at the same instant found himself wounded, turning round, he saw two Indians holding Magee and a third strike him with an axe, on the head—the Indian who shot the carpenter sprang to the boy, and with a dagger gave him a number of deep wounds in different parts of the body, notwithstanding which he got into the water and with the carpenter swam to a point of rocks in sight of the ship, the Indians immediately got into their canoe and left the cove, the people from the ship being alarmed, pursued them in a boat till they came to the spot where Magee lay weltering in his blood; they stopped and took him on board and on examining his wound, found his head was split across the left eye, he lived for 2 or 3 hours and then expired. The Boy had several deep wounds in his body, into which the salt water had found its way and in six hours he expired in excruciating agony—the escape of the Carpenter was a wonderful one—an Indian had stood directly over him and fired his pistol—the ball and 3 buck shots entered the upper part of his thigh and were afterwards extracted just above his knee—with this wound he continued to swim to a rock, was taken on board and recovered—the situation of the ship was now extremely critical. She was within musket shot of the woods in every direction except a narrow opening ahead, into which the wind blew directly—she was immedi-

ately hove off to her anchor—a hawser sent on shore and
bent to the long boat, by which means she was got off and
saved—the only way was now to endeavour to work out of
musket shot of the shore, while they were doing this the four
Indians had landed on the back side of the Harbour, came
over and began firing from the woods—one ball came
through the waist cloth and striking a man in the heart, killed
him instantly—several others were wounded- by the most
strenuous exertions this ship was at length got out clear and
left the place.

The second officer and two men belonging to the
Atahualpa were on shore at Chilcart and imprudently ate a
number of mussels, found on the beach—shortly after their
return on board they were seized with a sickness at the stom-
ach and swelling of the limbs—the officer and one man
immediately took an emetic and threw the poisonous matter
off their stomachs—the other neglected this precaution and
in a few hours expired in great misery—many of the mussels
found on the coast contain the most deliterious poison, but
the Indians distinguish them and eat the others without any
ill effects—among the other fortuitious events may be mentioned the loss of the Brig *Lavinia,* Captain Holbrook, on
her passage from Canton to America—she was spoken off
the Cape of Good Hope and was never heard of afterwards.
She had unfortunately been on the rocks on the N.W. Coast
and I presume was more injured than those aboard her were
aware of.

At the close of this season the N.W. Trade was at its lowest
ebb—the Indians had obtained such great quantities of
cloth, muskets etc. that they held these articles in very little
estimation—at Kigarnee and its neighborhood I have frequently seen the natives sell the sailors a fathom of blue cloth,
which cost not less than 3 dollars in America, for 5 biscuit
and a good musket for 10—this was not done from any
scarcity of provisions, but from their having a surplus of those

articles which they were at a loss what to do with—Rice, molasses and bread were the only articles in any sort of demand and but few vessels had any to dispose of.

1802

Description Vessells	Name	Masters	Where be-longing to	Number of Skins
Ship	*Globe*	Cunningham	Boston	3,500
"	*Atahualpa*	Wild	"	3,000
"	*Caroline*	Derby	"	3,000
"	*Manchester*	Brice	Philadelphia	300
"	*Alert*	Cobbetts	Boston	2,000
"	*Catharine*	Worth	"	1,200
Schooner	*Hetty*	Briggs	Philadelphia	500
Ship	*Jenny*	Crocker	Boston	500
"	*Vancouver*	Brown	"	14,000
"	*Juno*	Kendrick	" } Bristol } winter	

Sold at Canton for 20 dollars.

The *Unicorn*, Barber, went to Europe by the way of Cape Horn with 4 or 500 skins collected during the two seasons—business on the coast began to wear a rather more favorable aspect—yet still the price given for skins was enormously high—7 and 8 fathoms of blue cloth, with a number of small articles—muskets would not sell unless they were the best of Kings arms or handsome fowling pieces—Bread, Rice and molasses still held their value—none of the vessels which arrived this season had a sufficient quantity to meet the demand—Russia Sheeting was also in demand—a fathom of it being equal to a fathom of common blue cloth—their unreasonable prices were not given on all parts of the coast. At Newette, Millbank Sound and some parts of Queen Charlotte Islands, skins were procured on more favorable terms and at Newette four fathoms cloth with the usual small accompaniments, was given in the early part of the year—

towards the close the ship *Jenny* and schooner *Hetty* visited it
and very unnecessarily gave double that price—such an
uncommon influx of, what was by them considered as wealth,
brought with it its usual concomitants—luxury and want of
economy—many of the natives who were formerly contented
with one garment, now wore several and often changed from
for new ones—this in some measure counteracted the
ruinous effect which the exhorbitant price given for skins
would otherwise have had on the trade in future—the Indians, with that want of forethought natural to people in an
uncivilized state, did not reflect on the possibility of their
supplies hereafter being more limited and made no provision
against future wants—indeed, it was a very natural conclusion for them to draw, that the supplies furnished them
would continue to be as liberal as at present—they well knew
our sole motive for visiting them was, *ultimate gain*, by an
exchange of commodities and could not suppose we should
so entirely lose sight of the primary object of our voyage as to
give them more *actual value* for their skins than we could ever
expect to receive for them again—but they did not know that
some, who had the direction of this traffic, were scarcely
capable of making the most simple calculations and others
attended only to their own personal interest—without any
regard to that of their employers.

Several Gentleman from Philadelphia had made some
inquiries at Canton, respecting the N.W. Trade, and adopt-
ing the general opinion of its being very lucrative, they fitted
out the *Manchester* and *Hetty* with the most sanguine of
expectation, as I have since heard them declare, of rapidly
accumulating a fortune in the business.

The *Manchester* went to England and took in a very well
assorted cargo, with which she arrived on the Coast early in
1802. She was commanded by a Captain Brice, a man who
had passed his grand climacteric and had never been any
longer voyage than across the Atlantic—the officers were

drunkards and the crew mutinous and disorderly—the supercargo was a young man of talents, but without experience and not an individual on board had ever been on the coast before—thus situated, and the Captain and supercargo at variance, tis not to be supposed they could be successful— they cruised on the southern coast during the summer and wintered at Nootka Sound—here seven of the crew deserted and went on shore among the Indians, by whom they were afterwards massacred and devoured,—in Spring of this year they came to the Northward as far as Cumshawars on Queen Charlotte Islands, but a man of local knowledge and other circumstances prevented their meeting with any success and in July they proceeded to China with 200 skins, the sale of which and the remainder of her outward cargo not producing sufficient funds to pay the Port Charge. She was transferred to Wm. Berry at Canton—thus ended the first attempt of the Philadelphians to participate with the Boston merchants in the N.W. Trade.

The Schooner *Hetty* was rather more successful—she touched at the Sandwich Islands on her way to the coast— the Captain there engaged a man to go with him to the coast who had been there several times before—he first visited several ports on Queen Charlotte Islands in the Spring of this year where, finding the natives not inclined to sell their skins for the price offered he took the unjustifyable and pernicious method of using coercive measures to compel them to Trade. Several chiefs were seized and put in irons and obliged to deliver up all their skins, for which he gave them only what he pleased—these proceedings set all that part of the coast in a ferment—in April, Captain Briggs came into Kigarnee where was the *Vancouver, Caroline* and *Globe* and *Atahualpa* —the commanders of these vessels went on board, remonstrated with him on the impropriety of his conduct and threatened, if he persisted in such nefarious practices, to lend the natives every assistance in capturing him—he finally arrived at Canton with about 500 skins and made a ruinous voyage.

The ship *Truro* of Bristol (RI) arrived in July—she fitted out from England and part of her cargo was designed for the Spanish Coast—Captain Kendrick, who commanded her, was reported to be insane at intervals and all was confusion on board her—The cargo was well assorted and might have been sold to advantage—she went to the Sandwich Islands to winter; there Captain Kendrick was superseded in the command and left on shore—the vessel returned to the coast and eventually carried down 17 or 1800 skins, but made a sinking voyage.

I must now relate a transaction which attaches a very considerable share of blame to some of my countrymen—a transaction entirely repugnant to the dictates both humanity and policy, which, though it may in some measure be palliated, can by no means be justified—indeed it seems in this instance as though they had lost all sense of propriety, thrown aside the advantages of civilization and entirely exchanged characters with the ferocious savage.

In the year 1799, the Russians from Kamscatska had formed an establishment at Norfolk Sound, consisting of about 30 Russians and 7 or 800 natives of Kodiac and Onalaska for the purpose of killing sea otters and other animals—they had built a strong fort, contrary to the wishes of the native indians, who had, notwithstanding, conducted themselves in a peaceable manner, probably awed by the superior power of their new invaders—much to their discredit, the Russians did not adapt the same conciliatory conduct—but on some real or pretended suspicions of a conspiracy, pursued the most sanguinary course towards these people, some of whom were massacred and others sent in captivity to the Kodiac Islands. Stimulated to revenge by the loss of friends and relatives and, finding their source of wealth and almost of subsistence seized by strangers settled among them contrary to their wishes, the natives formed the plan of attacking the Fort and either extirpating their oppressors at a blow or perishing in the attempt—they succeeded, got possession of the fort by surprise and instantly put to death every man in the garrison—the Indian women, who were living with the Russians were made captives. The Kodiacs were at this time scattered about in hunting parties and became an easy prey to their more warlike opponents and some of them escaped in their canoes to the Russian establishments further north and others were killed or made slaves—antecedents to this, the ship *Jenny* of Boston had been at Norfolk Sound, where seven of her men deserted and took refuge with the Russians—the native Indians knew this and were willing to make a just distinction between those whom they considered as commercial friends and their arbitrary oppressors—they sent a message requesting the Americans to make them a friendly visit at their village—one of them accepted the invitation—the other was out with a party of Kodiacs hunting—when they arrived at the village the Indians communicated their designs and requested assistance—this, they of course declined giving—they were often assured that no injury should be offered *them*, but were at the same time informed they would be detained at the village to prevent any intimation being given to the Russians of what was in agitation—from the time of their successful attack on the Russians the Indians constantly protected and supplied the Americans till 2 American and one English ship came in about 20 days afterwards and they were then permitted to go where they chose—such conduct towards their countrymen merited the most friendly return from the Americans and policy as well as justice foiled any attempt to avenge the cause of the Russians—but unfortunately the commanders and officers adopted a different opinion—I am inclined to suppose they were, in this instance, too much influenced by the commander of the English ship, who was induced from

motives of interest to take part with the Russians—he was
bound to Kodiac and knew that whatever prisoners might be
rescued would be sent with him to the Russians settlements—this he expected would ingratiate him with the Russians and procure him some commercial advantages among
them—At a meeting of the officers of the different vessels it
was determined to seize the native chiefs who were along side
trading in the most friendly manner, and keep them as
hostages till the Kodiac women and other prisoners on shore
were delivered up—in pursuance of this resolve several, who
chanced to be on deck, were immediately secured, and an
attempt made to seize those in the canoes who fled for the
shore—they were fired on from the ships, and, to the eternal
disgrace of their *civilized* visitors, numbers were killed—the
first law of nature, self defence, justifyed to them returning
the fire, which they did, but without effect—the Captive
Chiefs were now told that unless all the prisoners on shore
were delivered up, they must expect no mercy (and it might
have been added, no justice)—they plead their utter inability
to comply with this requisition, as the prisoners were in possession of individuals over whom they had no authority—
one of the natives attempted to make his escape, but failed,
and in the attempt slightly wounded one of the ships company—he was immediately singled out as a proper object of
vengence and it was determined to sacrifice him, hoping by
that means to attain the object in view—a kind of mock trial
he was, in the true style of marine execution, placed on a log
on the forecastle, with a halter from the yardarm round his
neck, the gun fired and he hung up in the smoke of it—I cannot imagine the gentlemen could be so grossly ignorant of all
laws, human and divine as to suppose the formalities used on
this occasion could sanction an action at which humanity
shudders and justice stands appalled—one moments reflec-
tion must have told them that for this abuse of power, the
more amenable to the laws of their country, the strict letter of

which would condemn them to the same ignominious pun-
ishment they had inflicted on this unfortunate Indian—to
me their conduct appears inexplicable and will bear no com-
ments. Previous to his execution the Indian addressed them
in a speech of the following purport, which would have made
an impression on any not deaf to the cry of justice—"what
crime have we been guilty of to justify this wanton attack on
our liberty and lives—have we in any instance violated the
harmony hitherto existing between us—did we not on a late
occasion nicely discriminate between our commercial friends
and our invaders and cruel oppressors—when we sacrificed
the one to our just resentment—the other we protected, sup-
ported and on the first opportunity, restored to their country-
man—and is this the proper return for such conduct—you
say tis to revenge the massacre of the Russians and release the
prisoners that this attack is made—the Americans have
heretofore declared that the Russians were a distinct Nation
with whom they had no closer connections than with us if
that is the case, by what right do you interfere in the quarrel
betwixt us—when the Russians took numbers of our Tribe
and carried them into captivity—no one offered to rescue
them—your countrymen, tis true, reprobated the measure
and insinuated that we ought to take every precaution to prevent the Russians from establishing themselves among us—
this led us, rather, to view you as friends from whom we
might expect assistance, that as enemies who would oppose
us. If you persist in your present conduct, all friendly intercourse with us is at an end, for who will ever dare place any
confidence in people who have so grossly abused, as you have
in the present instance"—I have before observed that this
speech had no effect and the man was executed—after several days some of the Kodiac prisoners were liberated and put
on board the English vessel and sent to their former place of
residence.

The fate of the Norfolk Sound Indian was peculiarly distressing—in the summer of 1804 the Russians invaded them in great force—having with them a sloop of war which had come into these seas from Petersburg by way of Cape Horn—the Indians made a brave resistance and got possession of stockade or fort which they maintained for some time, but at length their ammunition being all expended and their numbers reduced, they determined to abandon their native shores and seek a retreat in the interior part of the country—in pursuance of this resolve they collected together and, shocking to relate, cut the throats of all the infants and old People of both sexes who were unable to support a journey through the desolate wilderness—choosing rather to massacre them with their own hands than suffer them to fall alive into the hands of their enemies from whom they expected no mercy—these particulars I had direct from the Commander of the Sloop of War who informed me that on landing to take possession of the fort he found it covered with the mangled bodies of the aged and innocent infants.

Captain Derby of the *Caroline* was left at the Sandwich Islands for the recovery of his health, but died there in September—the ship proceeded on for China.

A ship called the *Lois* sailed from Boston for the Coast, commanded by Captain Hawell—she touched at Rio Janeiro—left there—and was never heard of afterwards—tis thought she must have foundered off Cape Horn—I am entirely convinced she never arrived on the Coast, notwithstanding the confident operations to the contrary.

Account of the Vessels Engaged in the Sea-Otter Fur-trade on the Northwest Coast to 1808

In the following account of American vessels, it will be perceived that the latest date is 1807. From that time to the close of the War of 1812 the fur-trade was rather to be considered as the Columbia River trade, and the names of such vessels can be found in the text up to the time when Astoria was sold to the Northwest Company. I should have published a full list of the early traders to the Columbia, but could get no authentic statement.

List of American Vessels engaged in the Trade of the Northwest Coast of America for Sea-Otter Skins from 1787 to 1809, compiled by William Tufts, Esq., from his own Memoranda, and from the very valuable Notes kindly furnished by Captain William Sturgis, of Boston.

This document is from James G. Swan, *The Northwest Coast, or Three Years' Residence in Washington Territory* (1875; reprint, Seattle: University of Washington Press, 1972), pp. 423-25.

Time of sailing	Vessels' Names	Masters	Where owned	Owners	What Years on the Coast
1787	Ship *Columbia*	Kendrick	Boston	Barrell, Bulfinch & Co.	1788, 1789
1787	Sloop *Washington*	Gray	do.	do. do.	1788*
1788	None				
1780	None				
1790	Ship *Columbia*	Gray	do.	do. do.	1791, 1792†
1792	Sloop *Union*	Boyd	do	Not known	1793
1792	Ship *Jefferson*	Roberts	do		
1792	Brig *Hancock*	Crowell	do		
1792	Ship *Margaret*	Magee	do		}≠
1792	Brig *Hope*	Ingraham§	do		
1795	Snow *Sea Otter*	Hill	do		1796, 1797‖
1795	Schr.—	Newbury	do		1796
1796	Ship *Dispatch*	Bowers	do	Dorr and Sons	1797
1796	Ship *Indian Packet*	Rogers	do	do	1797
1796	Ship *Hazard*	Swift	do	Perkins, Lamb & Co.	1797, 1798
1797	Not known				
1798	Ship *Eliza*	Rowan	do	Perkins, Lamb & Co.	1799
1798	Ship *Ulysses*	Lamb	do	Lamb and others	1799
1798	Ship *Hancock*	Crocker	do	Dorr and Sons	1799
1798	Ship *Dispatch*	Breck	do	do	1799
1798	Ship *Dove*	Duffin	Canton	Not known	1799
1798	Ship *Cheerful*	Beck	do	do	1799
1798	Sloop *Dragon*	Cleveland	do	Cleaveland and others	1799
1799	Ship *Alert*	Bowles	Boston	Lamb and others	1800
1799	Ship *Jenny*	Bowers	do	Dorr and Sons	1800
1799	Ship *Alexander*	Dodd	do	Bass and others	1800
1799	Schr. *Rover*	Davidson	do	Dorr and Sons	1800
1799	Ship *Dove*	Duffin	Canton	....	1800
1799	Ship *Hazard*	Swift	Boston	Perkins & others	1800, 1801
1800	Ship *Charlotte*	Ingesoll	do	....	1801
1800	Ship *Guatimozin*	Bumstead	Boston	T. Lyman and others	1801
1800	Ship *Atahualpa*	Wildes	do	do	1801
1800	Ship *Globe*	Magee	do	Perkins, Lamb and others	1801, 1802*
1800	Ship *Caroline*	Derby	do	do do	1801, 1802†
1800	Ship *Manchester*	Brice	Philadel'a	....	1801, 1802
1800	Ship *Lucy*	Pierpont	Boston	Cobb and others	1801

Time of sailing	Vessels' Names	Masters	Where owned	Owners	What Years on the Coast
1800	Ship *Dispatch*	Dorr	do	Dorr and Sons	1801
1800	Ship *Belle Savage*	Ockington	do	J. Cooledge	1801
1800	Ship *Enterprise*	Hubbell	New York	Hoy & Thorn	1801
1800	Brig *Lavinia*	Hubbard	Bristol, R.I.	R.J. Dewolf	1801
1800	*Littiler*	Dorr	Boston	Dorr & Sons	1802
1800	Brig *Polly*	Kelly	do	Thomas Parish	1801
1801	Ship *Alert*	Ebbetts	do	Lamb and others	1802,1803
1801	Ship *Catharine*	Worth	do	J. Cooledge	1802
1801	Ship *Jenny*	Crocker	do	Dorr and Sons	1802
1801	Schr *Hetty*	Briggs	Philadel'a	....	1802
1801	Ship *Vancouver*	Brown	Boston	Lyman and others	1802,1803
1801	Ship *Juno*	Kendrick	Bristol, R.I.,	De Wolf	1802,1803
1802	Ship *Mary*	Bowles	Boston	J. Gray	1803≠
1802	Ship *Guatimozin*	Bumstead	do	Lyman & others	1803, 1804
1802	Ship *Hazard*	Swift	do	Perkins & others	1803,1804
1802	Ship *Boston*	Salter	do	T. Armory	1803§
1803	Ship *Atahualpa*	O. Porter	do	T. Lyman	1804,1805	
1803	Ship *Caroline*	Sturgis	do	Lamb and others	1804,1805
1804	Ship *Mary*	Trescott	do	J. Gray	1805
1804	Ship *Vancouver*	Brown	do	Thomas Lyman	1805,1806
1804	Ship *Pearl*	Ebbetts	do	Lamb and others	1805,1806
1804	Ship *Juno*	DeWolf	Bristol	DeWolf	1805
1804	Brig *Lydia*	Hill	Boston	T. Lyman	1805,1806
1805	Ship *Hamilton*	L. Porter	do	do	1806,1807
1805	Ship *Hazard*	Smith	do	Perkins &others	1806,1807
1806	Ship *Derby*	Swift	do	do do	1807,1808
1806	Ship *Guatimozin*	Glanville	do	T. Lyman	1807,1808*
1806	Ship *Atahualpa*	Sturgis	do	do	1807
1807	Ship *Pearl*	Suter	do	Perkins&others	1808,1809
1807	Ship *Vancouver*	Whittemore	do	do do	1808,1809

*Remained on the Coast under Captain Kendrick for many years. Gray went home in the Columbia; Kendrick was accidentally killed at the Sandwich Islands.

†Discovered Columbia River.

≠Time of sailing, time on the coast, and owners now known.

§Discovered the Washington Islands, South Pacific.

|Captain killed.

The number of sea-otter skins shipped from the North-west Coast to Canton in 1799 were 11,000

1800	9,500
1801	14,000
1802	14,000--48,500.

Mr. [William] Tufts writes, under date of Boston, February 3d, 1857,

"The foregoing list is nearly correct as it regards the vessels engaged in the early trade in *sea-otter skins* by American enterprise. The owners in all cases are not known. There may have been other vessels on the Coast during the time who were engaged in collecting the smaller skins and less valuable furs, but the above are the regular Northwest traders for sea otter skins.

"I have obtained the most of my information from Captain Sturgis, who very kindly gave me the information which his experience and notes rendered extremely valuable.

"We sailed from Boston (ship *Guatimozin*, Glanville) July 7th, 1806, arrived on the Coast March 20th, 1807, left the Coast September 24th, 1808, and were wrecked on the coast of New Jersey (on Seven-mile Beach) the 3d of February, 1810."

Mr. Tufts was supercargo of the ship.

It is a rather singular fact that some of the first furs ever carried to Canton direct from the Northwest Coast should have been by an American. Lieutenant John Gore, a native of Virginia, who was with Captain Cook, took charge of the expedition after the death of the captain at Karakoor Bay, Sandwich Islands, and Captain Clerke, who succeeded him, and who died at the Russian settlement of Peter and Paul, or Petropawlowsk. Gore sailed from Petropawlowsk, or, as the sailors call it at present, Peterpulaski, in October, 1779, and reaching Canton in the beginning of December. While the ships had been on the Northwest Coast, the officers and men had purchased a quantity of furs from the natives in exchange for knives, old clothes, buttons, and other trifles, not, however, with any reference to their value as merchandise, but to be used on board ship as clothes or bedding. On their arrival at Peterpulaski, they found the Russians anxious to buy all these furs; but, having learned that they were of great value in Canton, concluded to take them there, where they sold for money and goods for more than ten thousand dollars.

These furs, and a few carried by Benyowsky in 1770, were the only ones that had ever arrived at Canton direct from the Northwest Coast.

Bibliography

Bancroft, Hubert H. *The Northwest Coast* (vols. XXII and XIII, History of the Pacific States of North America). 2 vols. San Francisco: A.L. Bancroft & Co., 1894.

———. *History of California*. Vol. III (1825-40) (Works, vol. XX), San Francisco: History Co., 1886 (reprint, Santa Barbara, 1966).

Barragy, Terrence J. "The Trading Age, 1792-1844." *Oregon Historical Quarterly* 76 (1975): 196-224.

Bolkhovitinov, Nikolai N. *The Beginnings of Russian-American Relations, 1775-1815* (trans. Elena Levin). Cambridge: Harvard University Press, 1975.

Bradley, H.W. *The American Frontier in Hawaii, 1779-1843*. Palo Alto: Stanford University Press, 1942.

———. "Hawaii and the American Penetration of the Northeastern Pacific, 1800-1845." *Pacific Historical Review* 12 (1943): 277-86.

Busch, Briton C., ed. *Alta California, 1840-1842: the Journal and Observations of William Dane Phelps, Master of the ship ALERT*. Glendale, CA: Arthur H. Clark Co., 1983.

———, ed. *Frémont's Private Navy: the 1846 Journal of Captain William Dane Phelps*. Glendale, CA: Arthur H. Clark Co., 1987.

———. *The War Against the Seals: a History of the North American Seal Fishery*. Kingston and Montreal: McGill-Queen's University Press, 1985.

Caughey, John Walton. *Hubert Howe Bancroft: Historian of the West*. Berkeley: University of California Press, 1946.

Coghlin, Magdalen. "Boston Smugglers on the Coast (1797-1821): an Insight into the American Acquisition of California." *California Historical Society Quarterly* 46 (1967): 99-120.

_____. "Commercial Foundations of Political Interest in the Opening Pacific, 1789-1829." *California Historical Society Quarterly* 50 (1971): 15-33.

_____. "The Entrance of the Massachusetts Merchant into the Pacific." *Southern California Quarterly* 48 (1966): 327-52.

Cowdin, Elliot C., comp., "The Northwest Fur Trade" [Lecture by the Hon. William Sturgis]. *Hunt's Merchants' Magazine & Commercial Review* 14 (1846): 532-39.

Daws, Gavan. *Shoal of Time: A History of the Hawaiian Islands*. Honolulu: University of Honolulu Press, 1968.

Delano, Amasa. *A Narrative of Voyages and Travels in the Northern and Southern Hemispheres: Comprising Three Voyages Round the World* Boston: E.G. House, 1817; reprint, N.Y.: Praeger, 1970.

Dening, Greg. *Island and Beaches: Discourse on a Silent Land: Marquesas 1774-1880*. Honolulu: University of Hawaii Press, 1980.

Elliott, T.C. "John Meares' Approach to Oregon." *Oregon Historical Quarterly* 29 (1928): 278-87.

Fisher, Robin. "Arms and Men on the Northwest Coast, 1774-1825." *BC Studies*, no. 29 (1976): 3-18.

_____. *Contact and Conflict: Indian-European Relations in British Columbia, 1774-1890*. Vancouver: University of British Columbia Press, 2nd edition, 1992.

Gass, Ross H. *Don Francisco du Paula: A Biography and the Letters and Journals of Francisco de Paula Marin*. Ed. Agnes C. Conrad. Honolulu: University Press of Hawaii for the Hawaiian Historical Society, 1973.

Gibson, James P. *Otter Skins, Boston Ships, and Chinese Goods: the Maritime Fur Trade of the Northwest Coast, 1785-1841*. Montreal: McGill-Queen's University Press, 1992.

Gough, Barry M. "James Cook and the Origins of the Maritime Fur Trade." *The American Neptune* 38 (1978): 217-24.

_____, ed. *The Journal of Alexander Henry the Younger, 1799-1814*. 2 vols., Toronto: The Champlain Society, 1988, 1992.

_____. *The Northwest Coast: British Navigation, Trade and Discoveries to 1812*. Vancouver: University of British Columbia Press, 1992.

_____. *The Royal Navy and the Northwest Coast of North America, 1810-1914: a Study of British Maritime Ascendancy.* Vancouver: University of British Columbia Press, 1971.

Greenhow, Robert. *The History of Oregon California and the Other Territories of the North-west Coast of North America.* 3rd edition, revised. New York: D. Appleton and Co., 1845.

_____. *Memoir, Historical and Political, on the Northwest Coast of North America, and the Adjacent Territories.* Also printed under the same title, Washington: Blair and Rives, 1840.

Howay, F.W. *The ATAHUALPA which Vessel was Attacked by Natives on the Northwest Coast of America in June of 1805.* Fairfield, WA: Ye Galleon Press, 1978.

_____. "The Ballad of the Bold Northwestmen: an Incident in the Life Captain John Kendrick." *Washington Historical Quarterly* 20 (1929): 114-23.

_____. "Captains Gray and Kendrick: the Barrell Letters." *Washington Historical Quarterly* 12 (1921): 243-71.

_____. Captain Simon Metcalfe and the Brig ELEANORA." *Washington Historical Quarterly* 16 (1925): 114-21.

_____. "Early Days of the Maritime Fur Trade on the Northwest Coast." *Canadian Historical Review* 4 (1923): 26-44.

_____. "Early Relations between the Hawaiian Islands and the Northwest Coast." *Publications of the Archives of Hawaii* 5 (1930): 11-38.

_____. "The Fur Trade in Northwestern Development." In: H. Morse Stevens and Herbert E. Bolton, eds., *The Pacific Ocean in History* (N.Y., 1917), pp. 276-86.

_____. "The Introduction of Intoxicating Liquor amongst the Indians of the Northwest Coast." *British Columbia Historical Quarterly* (1942): 157-69.

_____. "Letters Concerning Voyages of British Vessels to the Northwest Coast of America, 1787-1809." *Oregon Historical Quarterly* 38 (1938): 307-13.

_____. *A List of Trading Vessels in the Maritime Fur Trade, 1785-1827.* Reprint from *Royal Society of Canada Transactions* (1931-4), Kingston: Limestone Press (ed. Richard A. Pierce), 1973.

_____. "An Outline Sketch of the Maritime Fur Trade." *Canadian Historical Association, Annual Report,* 1932 (Toronto, 1932): 5-14.

_____. *Voyages of the Columbia to the Northwest Coast 1787-1790 and 1790-1793.* Boston: Massachusetts Historical Society, 1944; reprint, Portland: Oregon Historical Society Press, 1990.

_____, ed. "William Sturgis: the Northwest Fur Trade." *British Columbia Historical Quarterly* 8 (1944): 11-25.

Ingraham, Joseph. *Journal of the Brigantine HOPE on a Voyage to the Northwest Coast of North America, 1790-92.* Ed. Mark D. Kaplanoff. Barre, MA: Imprint Society, 1971

Jewitt, John R. *The Adventurers of John Jewitt.* Ed. Robert Brown. London: Clement Wilson, 1896.

Kelley, Hall J. *Discoveries, Purchases of Land, etc. on the Northwest Coast Being Part of an Investigation of the American Title to the Oregon.* Boston: 1838.

Khlebnikov, K.T. *Baranov: Chief Manager of the Russian Colonies in America.* Trans. Colin Bearne; ed. Richard A. Pierce. Kingston, Ontario: Limestone Press, Materials for the Study of Alaska History, No. 3, 1973.

Kuykendall, Ralph S. *The Hawaiian Kingdom.* Vol. I: *"Foundation and Transformation, 1778-1854."* Honolulu: University Press of Hawaii, 1938.

Loring, Charles G. "Memoir of William Sturgis." Massachusetts Historical Society, *Proceedings,* 7 (1864): 420-73.

Meares, John. *Voyages Made in the Years 1788 and 1789, from China to the North West Coast of America.* London, 1790. Reprint: Amsterdam: N. Israel, 1967.

Mitchell, Donald H. "The Investigation of Fort Defiance: Verifications of the Site." *BC Studies,* no. 4 (1970): 3-20.

_____, and J. Robert Knox. "The Investigation of Fort Defiance: A Report on Preliminary Excavations." *BC Studies,* no. 16 (1972-73): 32-56.

Morison, Samuel Eliot. "Boston Traders in the Hawaiian Islands, 1789-1823." Massachusetts Historical Society, *Proceedings,* 44 (1920): 9-47.

_____. "The *Columbia's* Winter Quarters Located." *Oregon Historical Quarterly* 39 (1938): 3-7.

_____. *The Maritime History of Massachusetts, 1783-1860.* Boston; Houghton Mifflin, 1921.

Motteler, Lee S. *Pacific Island Names: a Map and Name Guide to the New Pacific.* Honolulu: Bishop Museum Press, 1986.

Ogden, Adele. *The California Sea Otter Trade, 1784-1848.* Berkeley: University of California Press, 1941.

Owens, Kenneth N., ed. *The Wreck of the SR. NIKOLAI: Two Narratives of the First Russian Expedition to the Oregon Country, 1808-1810.* Trans. Alton S. Donnelly, Portland: Western Imprints, the Press of the Oregon Historical Society, 1985.

Pethick, Derek. *First Approaches to the Northwest Coast.* Vancouver: J.J. Douglas, 1976.

Phillips, James W. *Washington State Place Names.* Seattle: University of Washington Press, 1971.

(Phelps, William D.) *Fore & Aft; or, Leaves from the Life of an Old Sailor, by Webfoot.* Boston: Nichols & Hall, 1871.

Prucha, Francis Paul. *American Indian Policy in the Formative Years: The Indian Trade and Intercourse Acts, 1790-1834.* Cambridge, MA: Harvard University Press, 1962.

Rich, E.E. *The Fur Trade and the Northwest Coast to 1857.* Toronto: McClelland and Stewart, 1957.

Richards, Rhys. *Captain Simon Metcalfe: Pioneer Fur Trader in the Pacific Northwest, Hawaii and China, 1787-1794.* Kingston, Ontario and Fairbanks, Alaska: Limestone Press, 1991.

(Sturgis, William.) *The Journal of William Sturgis.* Ed. S.W. Jackman. Victoria, BC: Sono Nis Press, 1978.

_____. "Examination of the Russian Claims to the Northwest Coast of America." *North American Review* 1822 (no. 36, n.s. 12): 370-401.

Swan, James G. *The Northwest Coast, or Three Years' Residence in Washington Territory.* [1875]; Seattle: University of Washington Press, 1972.

Tikhmenev, P.A. *A History of the Russian-American Company.* Trans. and ed. Richard A. Pierce and Alton S. Donnelly. Seattle: University of Washington Press, 1978.

Vaughan, Thomas, and Bill Holm. *Soft Gold: The Fur Trade and Cultural Exchange on the Northwest Coast of America.* Portland: Oregon Historical Society, 2nd. ed., 1990.

Weber, Francis J. *The Missions & Missionaries of Baja California.* Los Angeles: Dawson's Book Shop (Baja California Travels Series, 11), 1968.

Wheeler, Mary E. "Empires in Conflict and Cooperation: the 'Bostonians' and the Russian-American Company." *Pacific Historical Review* 40 (1971): 419-41.

Wright, E.W. ed. *Lewis and Dryden's Marine History of the Pacific Northwest.* Portland; Lewis & Dryden Printing Co., 1895.

Index